**Michael Paterson** is the author of *A Brief History of Life in Victorian Britain*, also published by Constable & Robinson.

Highlights from the series

*A Brief History of Roman Britain*
Joan P. Alcock

*A Brief History of the Private Life of Elizabeth II*
Michael Paterson

*A Brief History of France*
Cecil Jenkins

*A Brief History of Slavery*
Jeremy Black

*A Brief History of Sherlock Holmes*
Nigel Cawthorne

*A Brief Guide to Angels and Demons*
Sarah Bartlett

*A Brief History of How the Industrial Revolution Changed the World*
Thomas Crump

*A Brief History of King Arthur*
Mike Ashley

*A Brief History of the Universe*
J. P. McEvoy

*A Brief Guide to Secret Religions*
David Barrett

*His Finest Hour: A Brief Life of Winston Churchill*
Christopher Catherwood

*A Brief History of Witchcraft*
Lois Martin

# A BRIEF GUIDE TO
# PRIVATE LIFE IN BRITAIN'S STATELY HOMES

## MICHAEL PATERSON

RUNNING PRESS
PHILADELPHIA · LONDON

Constable & Robinson Ltd
55–56 Russell Square
London WC1B 4HP
www.constablerobinson.com

First published in the UK by Robinson,
an imprint of Constable & Robinson Ltd, 2012

All photographs are the author's own.

A copy of the British Library Cataloguing in Publication
Data is available from the British Library

UK ISBN 978-1-78033-689-3 (paperback)
978-1-78033-690-9 (ebook)

1 3 5 7 9 10 8 6 4 2

First published in the United States in 2012 by Running Press Book Publishers,
A Member of the Perseus Books Group

Books published by Running Press are available at special discounts for bulk purchases in the
United States by corporations, institutions, and other organizations. For more information,
please contact the Special Markets Department at the Perseus Books Group, 2300 Chestnut
Street, Suite 200, Philadelphia, PA 19103, or call (800) 810-4145, ext. 5000, or e-mail
special.markets@perseusbooks.com.

US ISBN 978-0-7624-4722-0
US Library of Congress Control Number: 2012931367

9  8  7  6  5  4  3  2  1
Digit on the right indicates the number of this printing

Running Press Book Publishers
2300 Chestnut Street
Philadelphia, PA 19103-4371

Visit us on the web!
www.runningpress.com

Typeset by TW Typesetting, Plymouth, Devon

Printed and bound in the UK

MIX
Paper from
responsible sources
FSC
www.fsc.org    FSC® C018072

This book is dedicated to Anne Roberts, my companion on many visits to country houses. A dear friend and ally, she also happens to be my mother-in-law.

As always, I thank my wife Sarah – not least for managing to re-start a defunct computer – and Dennis and Yvonne Cox, a charming couple, who provided some valuable information. I am also indebted to two dear friends, Grethe Hauge and Nora Relingh, for invaluable insights. Sharan Bhambra was immensely helpful in the final stages and I am very grateful. Both Duncan Proudfoot and Nicky Lovick at Constable & Robinson were a dream to work with.

Above all, I wish to thank my editor, Lynn Curtis, whose delightful sense of humour made her emails a pleasure to read. Her sympathy and patience went well beyond what I deserved.

It was a joy to share this project with all of them.

# CONTENTS

# PREFACE

We know the scene. It is August, and in the grounds of a country house a garden party is going on. It is a warm afternoon, but the cool shadows of the cedars are lengthening over the lawns. Violin music is coming from a marquee. Ladies with parasols and elaborate hats are strolling in the middle distance. The gentlemen wear frock coats despite the weather. Uniformed servants hover discreetly, offering refreshments. For backdrop there is the great house itself, home for centuries to a titled family. The Earl is talking to his guests. He is a man of decency and goodwill and strict fairness, benevolent ruler of his realm. His relatives are also decent and well-meaning and his servants, give or take the occasional crisis, are happy. Everyone knows their place, and appears content within it. The household runs like clockwork.

But amid the sunlight and music and the well-bred, inconsequential chatter, we see a figure approaching with measured tread. It is Carson the butler, and he carries a salver on which there is a telegram addressed to his master. It contains the news that the world has ended – or at least this version of it. The Earl opens the envelope, scans the contents with an expression of concern, and calls at once for silence. He tells the gathering that war has broken out in Europe. His guests look suitably disturbed. Some are even surprised.

This is the event that ends the first series of the television drama *Downton Abbey*. The announcement comes as no surprise to the television audience, which, forewarned by its knowledge of history, has been anticipating this moment for weeks. Indeed viewers are already in the habit of guessing which of the young men they have come to know from both above and below stairs are likely to survive the coming conflict, and when the female characters will be liberated from their various traditional roles by having to undertake war work. Those watching know that, from the moment the telegram is unsealed, the world will never be the same again. The parasols and the big hats will be put away for ever. Innocence has ended in the blink of an eye. We have crossed the fault line between the old world and the new, between the fairy-tale glamour of Edwardian high society and the horror of the trenches. Like the sinking of the *Titanic* with which the series began, the outbreak of war in August 1914 is a metaphor for Edwardian hubris, enabling scriptwriters to convey a sense of apocalypse – of thoughtless, extravagant hedonism, of the assumption of aristocratic superiority and an entire complex, fussy, snobbish and taken-for-granted social order, all coming to a sudden, crashing end. Some of those watching from their armchairs regret this, others think it about time.

Drama and history are not the same thing, however. The former, understandably, wishes to make events exciting: to play on the friction between different personalities, and the reaction of characters to circumstances that are unexpected and overwhelming. The reality of August 1914 was certainly dramatic, but it was very different. For one thing, it was not, properly speaking, the Edwardian era, which had ended with the death of Edward VII four years earlier. Much of the excess associated with his reign was by now a memory for the new king, George V, and his queen were seen as dull and worthy. Society was less frivolous and pleasure-seeking. Even women's dresses were more austere, angular, inelegant, than they had been a few years before.

It was not the case, as is so often implied in fiction, that the landowning aristocracy sat behind the walls of their estates with the smug sense that things would go on in the way they always had. These people were in crisis. Land – traditionally the source of their wealth and local prestige – had depreciated in value. They were increasingly unable to fill their servants' halls with people who 'knew their place' and, because they now had to pay National Insurance for each domestic employed, could no longer afford so many of them in any case. The landowning class was heavily taxed, and as a group had faced in recent years the hostility of a radical government. (There had recently been a proposal by the Liberals, only just deflected, to create up to 500 new peers, swamping the House of Lords and outnumbering the traditional aristocracy.) National politics was a poisonous two-way stand-off between the old and the new, Liberal and Conservative, that caused serious family rifts within the aristocracy itself. The suffragettes, whose campaign of vandalism and disruption was continuing unabated, had added a further element of instability and anarchy, with even ladies of good family landing in prison, deliberately or otherwise. In that summer of 1914 it was regarded as a certainty that civil war would break out in Ireland, within a matter of weeks or even days, over the issure of home rule. Both Protestants and Catholics there were forming military units, importing quantities of weapons, openly drilling and practising marksmanship. When this conflict broke out, it would cause further political division, and might even lead to the break-up of the United Kingdom.

In Europe, matters were even worse. Several times in recent years war between the major powers had almost broken out over some crisis or other. Now it had actually happened. In the space of a few weeks, between the end of June – when the heir to the throne of the Austrian Empire had been assassinated in Serbia – and the beginning of August, several nations had called up their reserves, closed their frontiers and begun hostilities. Things had come to a head on 1 August, when the armies of the German Kaiser had crossed the border into Belgium – a neutral country which Britain was pledged to protect – in order to attack France. Britons living on the Continent were fleeing in their thousands, abandoning businesses, education, holidays, so as to get home as quickly as possible. They were arriving in trainloads at Charing Cross and Victoria, dirty and exhausted and with tales of hostility and harassment and the horrors they had seen.

For Britain, the First World War did not begin at teatime on a sunny afternoon but at eleven o'clock at night, or midnight Berlin time, the hour at which an ultimatum from the British Government expired. Because the Kaiser had ignored a diplomatic request to withdraw his troops from Belgium, Britain declared war on Germany. In London on that warm evening Whitehall and the Mall were packed with people, converging on Big Ben to hear it ring out the end of peace, or on Buckingham Palace because that is where the British go at moments of high emotion. They had been waiting weeks to see if war would come, and if their country would be drawn into the approaching general cataclysm. During that time householders had been stockpiling food; young men as is implied in the series – were getting ready to enlist or had been training as Territorial soldiers; and many young women had already taken courses in nursing.

By the time of the fictional garden party at Downton Abbey, French, Belgian, Russian and German soldiers were already dying in heavy and desperate fighting, the first such major outbreak of hostilities in Europe since the Franco-Prussian War more than forty years previously. The whole of Britain was on a knife-edge. The guests would not have been surprised by the news, for they would have been talking of nothing else. But then, the event would have been cancelled in the first place, owing to the international situation.

In the years that would follow, many thousands of men of all social strata would serve in the war and would lose their lives. It is worth remembering that the upper class gave generously of its sons, for the young men who peopled the pre-war garden parties and hunting fields and college boat-races enlisted in droves. A single school – Eton – was to lose 1,157 of its Old Boys in the conflict. Women of this class, with a similar spirit of duty and self-sacrifice, joined a host of medical and charitable organizations, and either served in theatres of conflict or – as happens in the second series of the drama – gave their homes and resources to the war effort. The Edwardian upper class may often have exhibited a rather unconsidered sense of entitlement, but they were to prove a great deal less hedonistic than they seemed.

# INTRODUCTION

Let's imagine that you are visiting a medium-sized, somewhat typical country house, some time in the years just before the First World War. You are to be a guest for the weekend, though that term is not yet in use. At the moment it is still called a 'Saturday to Monday'.

You do not know your hosts well. They invited you to stay on the basis of some superficial meeting – perhaps after sitting next to you at a dinner and finding you'd never visited their part of the country. You have no notion of what to expect, but the address sounded suitably grand, and you have in your mind's eye an image of what their home will probably be like.

You would not – as people do today – drive yourself there as a matter of course. In those days the wealthy used public transport without a second thought, for even a small local train would have First Class carriages for them and Third Class for their servants. Upon your arrival at the station, a porter would immediately take your luggage and, on being informed of your destination, would tell you that the house had sent someone to fetch you. You would have let them know by telegram the time of your train's arrival, and with the efficiency you would take for granted a vehicle would have been dispatched to meet it. A few years earlier you would have been told that the coachman was waiting, and in the station yard would have been an open carriage, in some suitable colour such as dark green, dark blue, burgundy or canary yellow, with the family's coat of arms painted on the door. There would have been two servants: the coachman himself, in top boots, a top hat with a black cockade and perhaps a caped coat, and also a groom, similarly top-hatted and in livery, whose job was to help you into the carriage, shut the door and step up behind, to sit with arms folded on the dickey-seat throughout the journey. It is a sign of changing times that all this has gone.

Now there is only a motor car, painted black and with its engine spluttering. The only servant is the chauffeur, dressed in drab grey motoring clothes with leather gauntlets and leggings. He too wears a cockade, but it is on the front of a visored cap, above his goggles. You do not quite know how to deal with this unfamiliar type of servant. He deserves some respect for the technical knowledge that enables him not only to drive the thing – that in itself is as difficult as handling horses – but for his ability to understand the engine and to coax the vehicle into doing what he wants, since all motor cars are known to be temperamental. He seems to be a foreigner, for the French and Germans are more advanced in this field than the English, and when motor cars are bought abroad, a driver can be hired to come with them. His aloofness and mysterious knowledge probably make him unpopular among the other servants. Even a few years ago, at the beginning of the century, motoring was simply a hobby and an automobile was a rich man's toy. Now they are everywhere, and have almost entirely replaced the horse as a means of passenger transport. Streets in both town and country are simply full of them. There are very few horse-drawn cabs left – they are now a quaint curiosity – and the horse bus has almost entirely vanished. You cannot remember when you last saw one.

You are seated behind him with your own separate passenger's windscreen to keep the dust out of your face. Only you travel with him. Had you brought a servant they would follow with the luggage, which is coming in the station trap. It is pulled by a horse, for there is still a place in the modern world for such humble conveyances.

When you arrive at the entrance to the park that surrounds the house an elderly man will emerge, unsummoned (he has been watching, or perhaps the chauffeur has squeezed the rubber-bag horn to alert him), from the nearby lodge and heave open the big wrought-iron gates. He may greet the driver, whom of course he knows. He will also dip his head to you, and perhaps even make that immemorial gesture of subservience and touch his forelock.

Up the drive, between a double avenue of young trees, the house is visible, growing bigger and more imposing as you draw nearer. It is in the style irreverently known as 'Tudorbethan' – all quaint angles and gables. There are spindly, decorative brick chimney stacks, black and white half-timbering, swooping eaves, red tile roofs. Mullioned windows glint in the sunlight. Everything about it appears appropriately English, to the extent that it is almost a caricature. It evokes the world of Drake and Raleigh. You wonder if there is even a priest-hole, one of those hiding places for Catholic clergy that enabled families to practise the old faith in secret during Tudor times. It looks as if it has stood for half a millennium, yet you are to discover that it was built less than ten years ago. On closer examination, you can see that the brick and stone are not weathered and that there is not yet any sense of age to the building – in fact, through the stable-yard there is a glimpse of what looks like a garage, built in the same style. You are by no means disappointed, for you are aware that behind the mock-Tudor façade there is likely to be electricity and running water, and that for this reason it can be more pleasant to stay in a facsimile than in a genuine historic house. It is reassuring that you need expect no draughts, no noisy creaking floorboards, and no ghosts.

Whatever the age of the house, you know the sort of rooms it will contain. There will be a drawing room in which to sit out dances during a ball or to play bridge. There will be a dining room, perhaps hung with hunting scenes, in which a servant will stand behind your chair during meals. There may be a separate breakfast room in which the repast will be laid out on a sideboard under a row of silver dish-covers. There will be a library, either built up over generations and filled with interesting and valuable works or else 'bought by the yard', the leather spines being mere wall-covering. It may be the same with the pictures. Indeed the whole house could resemble a stage set in which nothing was actually chosen, inherited or treasured by the family, but simply put together by an interior decorator. It is comforting, however, to know that any self-respecting country-house library will boast two publications: annual runs of *Punch*, probably in matching bindings, and the equally uniform volumes of the Badminton Library – a Victorian-Edwardian series that explained the rules and intricacies of different games and sports. Both of these are old friends, and they will keep you entertained if the other guests prove uninspiring. It may be here that tea takes place each afternoon, unless there is a 'great hall' – one of those vast baronial rooms, all panelling and suits of armour, that even modern country houses sometimes have for the sake of appearance. This could well be the place in which the household gathers to hear important news. (Such as, in the yet-to-be written novels of Agatha Christie and Dorothy L. Sayers, who committed the murder!) If the owners are sufficiently devout, it could also be the setting for daily prayers at which family, guests and servants assemble.

In ironic contrast to this hint of piety there will be a billiard room and a smoking room. This last is a comparatively new feature, having come into vogue only in the last half century. It is an entirely masculine domain, habitually decorated with the trophies of male sporting pursuits: stuffed fish, heads of game, and photographs of sports teams. It is here that men can entirely relax, and tell the kind of stories that are not acceptable in mixed company. These places feature extensively in the novels of John Buchan, as the setting in which his upper-class heroes plan their adventures. Women do not enter this room, and they will not do so even after the Great War, when so many conventions are thrown overboard and it becomes common practice for females to smoke in public. The gentlemen's smoking room is an institution that will endure for a long time. When one Scottish house was taken over by a new family as recently as the 1970s, it still had a smoking room in which no woman had ever set foot. When the wife of the new owner went into it, the female housekeeper was horrified enough to resign at once.

If you are a single man, you may be fervently hoping that in one sense at least your hosts will not stick too closely to tradition. The rooms occupied by some of the 'upstairs' people in a house like this may be little better than the servants' quarters. Foreign visitors to British houses mention that for unmarried male guests it is not thought necessary to give them anything much in the way of comfort, and that the 'bachelors' wing' of a house can often contain poky, sparsely furnished and unheated rooms that are much the same as those slept in by the maids.

The children, incidentally, are also housed in spartan conditions. When visitors today look into the nurseries of Victorian country houses they may admire the expensive toys – the Noah's arks and rocking horses and tin soldiers – but they are seldom impressed by the rooms themselves. Once again, it was considered unnecessary to provide beauty or comfort for this category of the house's inhabitants. Sometimes there are decorative friezes or other touches of colour, but the décor in many pleasant nurseries (the one at Wightwick Manor in

Staffordshire is a good example) dates from a later era. The children's rooms were traditionally also far removed from those of their parents.

But to resume . . . Between the trees you can already see the flashes of white – glimpses of cap and apron – that show the servants are assembled to greet you. Your progress will have been watched as you travelled up the drive.

As the vehicle comes to a halt outside the main doors, its wheels crunching on the gravel, you see the whole household standing in position. They are in two rows, either side of the entrance, and are arranged in order of seniority with the most junior – the page – nearest you. You scarcely notice the latter as you pass, for such small fry are not the servants who will be waiting upon you. He in turn may have little interest in you, for very junior servants are not the ones who will benefit from any tips you give. One of his tasks is to clean the shoes of the household, but you will be assigned a personal servant and they will do this for you. The butler and house-keeper, the highest-ranking staff, are farthest away, and the family themselves are framed in the doorway. The chauffeur climbs down, pulls off goggles and gauntlets, and opens the door, helping you down the single step. As you approach, the maids in their black-and-white uniforms drop a simultaneous curtsy, the male servants in their brass-buttoned tail-coats bow.

It all looks just as you knew it would.

Beyond the doorway, after you have been greeted by your hosts, servants have bustled in to relieve you of your coat, hat and other accoutrements. You have now seen all of the domestics, so their faces will in future be familiar. That was the point of parading them all. You are next introduced to the one who will be tending to your needs during your stay. It will be a lady's maid, or a footman acting as valet, depending on your gender. They will show you to your room, see to your unpacking, run you a bath, lay out your clothes and dress you for tea or for dinner. They will wait in the passageway outside in order to accompany you downstairs and prevent you from losing your way, and they will serve you whatever you are to eat. They will also acquaint you with any quirks or customs of the house that may be unfamiliar, such as how and when the signal is given to change for dinner. They will awaken you the following morning by gently drawing the curtains of your room, and they will bring you tea on a tray, together with a newspaper that has been ironed.

Those who live here, whether they are members of an ancient family whose roots are sunk deep in the local soil or – as was all too common by the Edwardian era – *arrivistes* like your putative hosts, will conform to a particular style of dress and manners. You knew this the instant you saw them assembled at the entrance to greet you, surrounded by lolling dogs. The husband and the grown-up sons are in tweeds and are smoking pipes. The wife and daughters are also in tweeds, for it is autumn and the costume of country gentlewomen is briskly practical too. These of course will be changed for white tie and décolletage respectively in time for dinner. When this has ended the men will linger in the dining room over port and cigars and discussion of politics before joining the ladies in the drawing room. In mixed company, the talk will be of hunting and shooting – for those who have the facilities for these seldom fail to practise them, and the season for both has now begun – of visits to Cowes or Henley, Homburg and Baden-Baden or Monte Carlo. The sons may be home for the holidays from boarding school or Oxford. The daughters may be preoccupied with thoughts of next year's London Season. There is a code of behaviour, a series of expectations, amounting to a complete lifestyle that goes with life in an English country house, and everyone, from the scullery maids to the owner, knows what is involved. Often those who are new to wealth and gentility will be the most punctilious in keeping up standards, partly because they wish to endorse a world they have worked so hard to enter, and partly because they are afraid of making mistakes or showing that they do not 'know the form'.

Provided you are at home in this world – if, in other words, you understand the etiquette, know what to change into and when, whom and how much to tip – you will experience a level of service and comfort that will make this one of life's pleasantest interludes. The year of your visit, no matter which it is, will be a time of anxiety. Politically speaking, these are frantic, dangerous years, and it is ironic that history should remember them as sunlit and leisured. It is naturally understood that you keep away from political discussion in public (this will only take place between the men after the ladies have left them following dinner), but everyone of this class can be assumed to share the same sense of outrage at the Liberals and exasperation with the Conservatives, and the subject is bound to come up for half a dozen reasons, not least for the fact that servants are becoming more expensive. It is wisest just to take your cue from your hosts, and agree with any opinions they express.

You meet the other guests. They too are much as you expected: a few old friends of the family, a young man who is engaged to one of the daughters, a soldier returned from the Colonies, an old aunt who is hard of hearing, and some City men and their wives. No one very interesting, but that does not matter. Though you must make an effort with them during meals, and play the odd hand of bridge to show willing, you can amuse yourself in solitude if you prefer. There are walks to be had around the estate during the day, and there is the library for the evenings. It is well known that an ideal house guest is one who will find things to do and not get under the feet of their hosts, having to be talked to and entertained all the time.

If you wish to stay in your room you can therefore do so without being considered antisocial. If you want to be alone you can say that you must write letters. This is a catch-all excuse to get out of uncongenial circumstances, especially if you are a woman, for they seem to spend hours every day at this task. Though the telephone and the telegram are both widely in use for the sending of urgent messages, all other news is conveyed in notes and letters. Victorians and Edwardians, with their swift and cheap postal service, were in any case inveterate letter-writers. Frequent practice made them eloquent, and many thousands of them could draw well enough to illustrate their narratives. They wrote to each other with the same regularity that people now send e-mails. The author John Buchan, as an ambitious young Oxford man beginning to do the rounds of country houses in the

1890s, wrote to his mother without fail every day, in addition to studying for a degree, corresponding with numerous other people, writing books and producing reviews and articles for magazines.

Love of solitude was even more acceptable in earlier generations, before the railway had quickened the pace of life by making the flying, weekend visit possible. Those who stayed at country houses in previous centuries were often there for weeks, and perhaps even months. With no structured activities or sense of purpose, and the same company day after day, this must have become an ordeal. It was therefore acceptable to seek diversion on one's own account. One thinks of Fanny Price, the heroine of Jane Austen's *Mansfield Park*, who shut herself away for long periods in her room because she did not approve of the other guests' desire to put on an amateur play, and read her way through Lord Macartney's memoir of his diplomatic visit to China. Where a house boasted a good library and the guests were sufficiently curious and intelligent, there was nothing blameworthy about reading for long hours at a time. Your host might even take it as a compliment.

So if you have no worries about saying or doing the wrong thing, possess enough knowledge of culture to appreciate paintings or to be impressed by the library, know enough about horses and field sports, play bridge well enough and are able to keep your end up in superficial conversation throughout long afternoons and even longer evenings – and especially if you have the good manners to be interested in the garden – you will feel at home no matter how far away you actually live. There is, as we have seen, a code of conduct common to these families and their homes, which varies only in the finer details from place to place. If you understand it, you belong.

What you naturally do not know, as you sip tea on the terrace or tour the stables with your host, is how quickly this way of life will soon vanish. Nobody else realizes this either, which is surprising. The landowning class which inhabits houses like this includes politicians, captains of industry and newspaper proprietors, who are the best-informed and most influential people in the country. They are aware of how fast the world is changing, and they know that a war is likely to come at some time in the next few years, but what they and their peers do not appreciate is that this event will rob them almost entirely of those who maintain their homes and comforts. Their domestic staff will soon be melting away into the armed forces or war work, and for most households it will not be possible to reassemble them again. The war will cause not only terrible loss of life but a major change in social attitudes. Those members of the servant class who survive the conflict will in many cases be unwilling to return to the life they previously led.

But that is in the future. For the present, you may enjoy your surroundings and the comfort that goes with them. At the time of your visit the best conditions prevail. There is as yet no shortage of servants. In fact, there are far too many for you to remember all their faces. They are everywhere, doing everything for you. At the same time the house, like many other spacious and modern country houses, is more agreeable to live in than at any other time, for in less opulent decades the maintenance and the heating of them will become prohibitively expensive. Now there is electricity, the telephone, hot running water, and a host of amusements. Modern technology has added an entire new layer of comfort to that already supplied by numerous willing hands, so that you are much better off than your grandparents would have been when staying at a country house half a century earlier. You are in the twilight of a golden age. And as is always the case, you will not know it was a golden age until it is over.

# I

# THE BRITISH COUNTRY HOUSE

'Of all the great things that the English have invented and
made part of the credit of the national character, the most
perfect, the most characteristic, the only one that they
have mastered completely in all its details so that it
becomes a compendious illustration of their social genius
and their manners, is the well-appointed,
well-administered, well-filled country house.'

Henry James, *English Hours*, 1905

Why does the world of the British country house so
fascinate us? Most of us have no experience of living in
one, though we visit in our millions the 'stately homes'
that are open to the public. In the collective conscious-
ness both of the British themselves and those who visit,
or even visualize, the British Isles, the rural gentleman's
seat – the country house, the stately home – is a
repository of all that is finest in life: artistic treasures,

good manners, good food (if you're lucky), good taste in its furnishing and decorations, hospitality, and memory. Like the parish church that so often stands nearby, it is a storehouse of local lore and history; a self-contained world that defies – or at least gives the impression of doing so – the changes taking place beyond its walls. About its restful rooms and lawns there is a sense both of timelessness and of time passing; of ancient secrets. One such house, Snowshill Manor in Gloucestershire, which dates from around 1500, has an inscription that perfectly conveys this:

> Old I am, so very old,
> Here centuries have been.
> Mysteries my walls enfold,
> None know deeds I have seen.

Joanna Martin, whose family are the owners of Penrice Castle in Wales, also summed up this sense of the passing ages while writing the preface to a journal she had discovered there and sent for publication:

> The house was built in 1770 and has never been sold. This means that nobody has ever thrown away the miscellaneous debris of family life. I would open a drawer in the old nurseries and find a half-finished piece of sewing, which had been put away and forgotten almost 200 years before. In the next drawer I might find a piece of tissue paper, containing locks of hair from the heads of long-dead ancestors.

The notion of a country house as a sort of giant lumber room filled with curiosities is not the least agreeable aspect of these places. An outstanding example of this was Calke Abbey in Derbyshire, home for four centuries to the Harpur-Crewe family. When it came to public notice in 1981 because it was about to be sold, it had been left effectively untouched since the reign of Victoria. Family members who had owned it over generations had been unwilling or unable to install modern heating or lighting, and had inhabited only some of its rooms. The result was a treasure trove – a sort of Tutankhamun's tomb – of art and furniture, costume, vehicles, domestic clutter, children's toys, stuffed birds, and the type of eccentric 'curiosities' dear to the hearts of nineteenth-century collectors. The new owner – the National Trust, which was able to rescue house and contents for the public – ensured that in some rooms the jumble of piled-up objects would not be tidied away until it had been extensively photographed. People were enchanted by the sense of random historic disorder.

It is important that country houses should not be too tidy, too antiseptic, too recently restored, or indeed too overwhelming. Though visitors can be impressed by the scale and grandeur of Blenheim Palace, whose complex of buildings is the size of a small airport, they are unlikely to be charmed, or to want to live there. It is all too big, and it looks too uncomfortable. The ideal house should fit into the surrounding landscape and – whether it is Tudor, Palladian or neo-Gothic – should have a certain architectural understatement. Inside, it is important that it should look lived in. There should be a certain comfortable raffishness – a patina suggesting that it is well used and well loved, somewhat faded and comfortably down-at-heel. Visitors like to see evidence that family life continues amid the ancestral portraits and the suits of armour. At one Scottish house, Scone Palace in Perthshire, a guide pointed out a stain on the ceiling caused by a washing machine overflowing in the room above. Toys piled in a corner ('We've got one of those!' someone will often exclaim), some unfinished embroidery or even the television listings left conveniently on a table, will all add to the sense that this historic house is still a home. Where family photographs are displayed, regular visitors will take an interest in the children over the years and will ask what they are up to now. The owners know all this, and like to emphasize that their house is just like ours, though perhaps older and on a larger scale. As the guidebook to one spectacularly lovely dwelling, Deene Park in Northamptonshire, puts it: 'Although it has never been a house full of famous and priceless treasures it is a very much loved home which has been lived in by the same family [the Brudenells] for over 400 years.'

It is assumed, and not without sympathy, by many of those who wander around that the owners of these properties have to struggle to keep them going. For every visitor who envies the space they enjoy or the things they have inherited, there will be others who give thanks that they do not have to pay for the maintenance. There is, in other words, remarkably little resentment felt today towards those who own and inhabit country houses. Indeed, visitors will often donate more than they are asked for, or spend heavily in the gift shop.

Country houses can, in any case, belong to people other than those who own them. If you visit one regularly, it becomes part of your personal landscape. If you marry in one – and many can now be hired as wedding venues – it becomes part of your family history. And of course not all of them are in private hands anyway. In the 1950s an American author, Ruth McKenny, visited Newstead Abbey, a Tudor house near Nottingham that was once the ancestral home of Lord Byron. It had already been owned for decades by the city and used as a public park. She watched, on a Sunday afternoon, 'the coal-miners and factory-hands of Nottingham stroll through the perfumed rose-gardens' and examine 'with a pleased and expert eye the Japanese dwarf water-gardens'. She went on to observe that Newstead was 'one place where the people of England have inherited the past they made with their sweat. The great-great-grandchildren of the peasants [whom the Byrons employed to lay out the park] sit, arm-in-arm with their girls, or their beaux, in the Grecian summer-house, sighing over the romantic vista of water and lawn.' It is not only the wealthy and aristocratic who can enjoy a glimpse of Arcadia.

An old country house (because not all of them are very old, by British standards) will have been the centre of local life for centuries. It is more common than we might suppose to find families who have lived in the same house, or at least one on the same site, for seven or eight hundred years. Generations of them may be interred beneath marble effigies in the nearby church, in which they will have built their own chapel for this purpose. As well as farming their estate, they will have served as Lords-Lieutenant and High Sheriffs of the county, Members of Parliament, Masters of Fox Hounds, officers in the local Yeomanry, and perhaps even as rectors of the church itself. Thus their lives are extensively entwined with the surrounding area. They will have a lasting local fame – or notoriety – even if their names are unknown to a wider public.

Their servants, too, represent another form of continuity, for local people will have been the most ready source of labour for as long as the house has stood, and the neighbourhood is likely to abound with families whose aunts and uncles and grandparents were gardeners or maids or coachmen in the big house. The descendants of these people may hold the same, or similar, positions today, or they may have jobs on the estate that did not exist in the old days – as staff in the tearoom or the gift shop (or even the safari park!), or as part-time volunteers showing visitors around. They have an emotional stake in the house and, again, a sense that it belongs to them too. If it is well enough known to attract multitudes of tourists through its collections, its associations with famous people or events, or through having appeared on film or television, it can represent a significant element in the local economy.

Is it only the British who have this passion for country houses? Is it only they who dream of one day living in a castle or a manor house or a Palladian mansion? Absolutely not. The same desire is found in virtually every country, for the British have no monopoly on gracious rural living. In other cultures there are equivalent places: the *château* in France, the *schloss* in Germany, the *dvor* in Poland, the *estancia* and the *hacienda* throughout the Spanish-speaking world. All these terms mean the same thing: a castle or an estate. A house surrounded by land. They can be emotive terms in their different languages, encapsulating a concept that appeals to a common sense of nostalgia and tradition.

One thing that made British country estates significantly different from those on the Continent, however, was the custom of primogeniture. In other countries, all the sons of a count or baron would become counts or barons too. In Britain only the first son would inherit the title, while his brothers were awarded some lesser appellation. By the same token only the eldest son would inherit the family lands, while the others generally inherited none. However unfair from their perspective, this meant that estates remained intact, not diminishing in size through the generations and centuries, as was often the case elsewhere. The alternative, widely seen in other societies, was that estates dwindled through constant subdividing between siblings. The family's holdings remained the same, but often could not be farmed in a coordinated manner because there was confusion or failure to agree between all the owners. This gave the great British country houses a majesty, a power and a wealth that their counterparts elsewhere often could not match.

There are many country houses built on the English pattern in the United States, especially along the eastern seaboard. The homes of older American families, in Virginia, Georgia, Massachussetts or upstate New York, tended to be relatively unostentatious and modest in scale, however, and the really great houses – such as the Vanderbilt family's Biltmore in North Carolina – belong to a more recent era (it was built between 1888 and 1895). These newer houses were therefore able to exist in the

'grand manner' for no more than three or four generations before the age of splendour and large staff came to
an end. Though they are undoubtedly pleasant to look at
and interesting to visit, they cannot compete with their
long-established counterparts across the Atlantic.

In Europe there are, naturally, houses as ancient and
as famous. The *châteaux* of the Loire Valley in France
exceed in grandeur all but the greatest of English country
houses, such as Burghley House in Lincolnshire (1558–
87) and Wilton House in Wiltshire (*c.*1630–55). But then
a certain modesty and 'homeliness' is something that
adds to the appeal of many British stately homes.

What makes them different is their informality. In the
eighteenth century their grounds were laid out not in
rigid, geometrical parterres on the French model but as
'wild' meadow-like spaces, suitable for hunting, riding,
walking. They became places for relaxation and not a mere
backdrop for display by strutting, strolling aristocrats.

The contents of many British country houses accumulated over generations because after the English Civil
Wars (1642–51) the United Kingdom was largely peaceful. There were no events dramatic enough to disperse
both occupants and their possessions, as happened so
often on the Continent. It is somewhat surprising to
reflect that, for a country so active in world affairs and
one that has been for centuries a major military power,
Britain has been internally at peace for over 250 years.
The last battle to take place on mainland British soil was
as long ago as 1746, and that was in the far north of
Scotland. For centuries no wars, revolutions, peasant
uprisings or occupations by foreign powers have disturbed the peace of British parklands, though estate walls

have not protected the occupants of great houses from economic slump and punitive taxation, which have sometimes proved to be as dangerous as weaponry.

The same cannot be said for many other corners of Europe. Even Scandinavia, considered a peaceful region, received the attentions of Peter the Great, Napoleon and Hitler. Most of central Europe suffered widespread devastation in the Thirty Years War (1618–48), a level of destruction that was not to be seen again until the 1914–18 conflict. France and Belgium saw most material damage in those latter years, while Italy was extensively fought over in the Second World War. The one truly neutral country, Switzerland (though invaded by Napoleon) had no aristocracy.

In Poland, Russia and parts of the old Habsburg Empire in central Europe, the scale of destruction was often massive. In the Russian countryside the local manor house was frequently a target for revolutionaries, and the fact that these dwellings were often built of wood made them easier to burn. A member of one landed family, returning to look for his forebears' home after the end of Communism, found the park in which it had been set but not a trace of the house itself. He discovered the 'footprint' of the building only because of the surviving flower beds that had once surrounded it. When a house was left standing, it was emptied of its contents, which, if valuable, were hived off to museums and State collections, for in these countries it was illegal for citizens to own antiques. One Czech member of a landed family walked through the empty rooms of his ancestral castle in the 1990s, telling a British interviewer that only Western countries could afford to take for granted a sense of continuity with the past. Over the centuries his family had, he remarked laconically, lost everything no less than seven times.

In Germany the area containing the biggest landed estates – the Junker heartland of East Prussia – was right in the path of the advancing Russian armies in 1945. Aristocrats there were doubly hated by the conquerors as both ideological (fascist) and class enemies. Those who stubbornly refused to flee their homes could do nothing to protect their belongings or their position, and faced the bleak choice between harassment and imprisonment or death. Typical of them was a daughter-in-law of Otto von Bismarck, Germany's 'Iron Chancellor', who stayed at her family estate of Varzin and made preparations to kill herself before the Russians reached the gates. Countess Marion Donhoff's memoir, *Before the Storm*, records:

> No amount of warnings and arguments would persuade her to leave Varzin. She had no illusions about surviving the entry of the Russians, nor did she want to witness it. She had had a grave dug in the garden, for she assumed that later on nobody would have time to do so. Her old butler . . . also refused to leave.

Even the Irish Republic, so close to Britain that it shares the United Kingdom's only land border, has not been as peaceful. The War of Independence and subsequent Civil War (1918–23) saw the abandonment or destruction of country houses as conspicuous symbols of rule by a foreign aristocratic caste. Similar troubles during the nineteenth century had already put a number of rural houses into a state of siege (defensive rifle-slits can still be seen in the walls of some). The owners of many big houses, either burned out or feeling that they did not fit into the new Ireland, sold up and left. For many decades after Independence, the republican orthodoxy of the Irish Government prevented funds being used – or legislation passed – to preserve or protect country houses. Many were put to other uses, demolished, or simply left to fall down.

This situation, though serious, was not the whole picture, however. There had been no policy in Ireland of banishing or persecuting the aristocracy as there had been after Communist takeovers, and a number of titled men served the new Republic as Senators. Others have lived undisturbed in the country ever since – the Dukes of Devonshire and Westminster, for instance, continue to occupy their families' Irish homes. Nevertheless 'the Troubles' saw a significant break with the past and the dismantling of many private estates through confiscation and nationalization.

So Britain became by default a rare, if not quite unique, place of stability within the context of European aristocracy. It is not simply this, however, that has cast the common perception of the British country house in such an idyllic light. The British have shown a particular genius for creating gardens and interiors that are elegant yet comfortable, ostentatious yet understated, which is envied – and copied – throughout the world, and only the British have made their country houses into a major literary genre.

And then there are their servants. It would somehow be unthinkable that in other countries a butler (and this functionary is an English invention; in Europe he would be called a steward) could achieve the status in popular culture enjoyed by Jeeves and his confrères. The notion of a servant – even a senior one – occupying a position of benevolent influence over his employer, in the way that P. G. Wodehouse's character does, would be unusual to say the least in many other countries.

Interest in the British class system is responsible for much of the fascination that greets films and books in this genre abroad. Many equivalent societies in Europe or America are not nearly so structured, so precise, so preoccupied with social status. Some places, like Scandinavia or the Netherlands, are too easy-going to have developed the type of social stratifications the British have. In others, such as Germany or Austria, these would historically have been even more pronounced, but those countries officially lost their monarchies and aristocracies almost a century ago, and social changes since then have ensured that this class will never again exert power in what are now bourgeois republics.

Even in the Germany of Wilhelm II or the Austria of the Habsburgs there was, in any case, no particular accent that divided the upper classes from everyone else. In Britain speaking 'correctly' was a badge of belonging, as was being educated at a school for the privileged that might be hundreds of miles from one's home. As were the sports and games one pursued, or the quality of world-famous English tailoring that one wore. In many aspects of gentility it was Britain that set the tone, while the rich and aristocratic of other countries either followed or shook their heads in despair at the lunacy of it. The United Kingdom was the fountainhead of much that was fashionable in the nineteenth and early twentieth centuries, but equally of much that was considered eccentric, peculiar, funny. People throughout the world continue to find the British upper class amusing, not least because it is so superbly good at making fun of itself. Of novelists who have successfully dealt with this subject, either satirically or as a cultural phenomenon, all have been Britons themselves except for one: Kazuo Ishiguro, the Japanese author of *The Remains of the Day.*

And in other countries there is just not the same fascination with aristocratic concerns. A Dutchwoman once commented to me that in her country popular culture was only interested in the stories of 'ordinary people', while a Dane took the view that because class distinctions were so much less precise there, writers or producers simply could not create a dramatic enough plot.

For the United States, of course, British history is the prelude to its own, and after Independence it is a matter of peoples following different paths. America, committed from its inception to republican ideals, would not have allowed the emergence of an openly aristocratic class, despite the fact that it has had the wealth and the institutions and the opportunities to do so. Nevertheless, without ever wishing to have such a system of landowning based on feudal practices or all the complexities of ceremonial titles for themselves, many other countries and societies can enjoy these things at a distance through the country-house creations of British authors and dramatists.

The 'stately homes of England' have been a staple of fiction for centuries, from the days of Henry Fielding and Jane Austen to Evelyn Waugh in the early twentieth century and *The Remains of the Day* at the end of it. *Downton Abbey*, of course, is the twenty-first century's take on this perennially fascinating topic. They have provided locations for plays, opera (Henry James' short novel *The Turn of the Screw* was adapted by Benjamin Britten), and numerous body-in-the-library murder mysteries as well as more serious literary works such as *Atonement*, *The Shooting Party*, *The Last September*, *Brideshead Revisited*, *Good Behaviour* and *Troubles*. In the first half of the twentieth century there was even an entire theatrical genre – that of 'drawing room comedy' – devoted to the behaviour of polite, upper-class folk in the surroundings of opulent houses. In other words, it is clear that during the very decades later regarded as the heyday of the country house, it was equally revered in contemporary culture. This great era of country-house living has, in our own time, been the subject of major films and television programmes besides *Downton Abbey*, and public interest shows no sign of flagging.

As we wander the rooms and gardens of houses that we visit, it tends not to be the present-day life of the household on which we dwell. Instead our imagination will often take us – by express lift, as it were – straight to the world of the Victorians and Edwardians. Even if the house itself is much older, it is this era that will command our interest, for the century before 1914 is seen as the golden age of country-house living, the time in which these splendid settings came into their own. It is this period with which we are most familiar, and of which we think at once when the notion of a grand house comes to mind because, as we have seen, it was in these eras that country houses achieved an unsurpassed level of opulence and formality.

There were more country houses during this period than ever before or since. Britain gained vast wealth in the nineteenth century. Though agriculture suffered a huge decline, industry and commerce produced an echelon of new millionaires who aped the lifestyle of the old aristocracy, among whom a country estate became an important badge of belonging. Encompassing every degree of taste from elegant to hideous, new baronial-style dwellings sprouted in every corner of the British Isles. Though it is the *English* country house about which one so often hears, it is worth remembering that many of the best examples – the most gracious, or extravagant, architecture, the most immense estates, the wealthiest families, the most historic or romantic houses – are not in England at all but in Scotland or Ireland, and that in these countries there are many more of them. In the Deeside region of Scotland alone there are 35 castles.

The aristocracies of Scotland and Ireland were in no sense separate from that of England. They were related through innumerable marriages. They attended the same schools and universities (usually in England). They met in London because they rented houses there for the Season. They took part in the round of sporting and social events that every summer drew the wealthy and fashionable to parts of southern England, but in August, when the time arrived for deer stalking and grouse-shooting, it was the English aristocracy that trekked to Scotland. The British upper classes were completely integrated, regardless of where in the realm they lived.

There was much more to do in these houses too, and

as the nineteenth century wore on the railway made them easier to visit. Electricity and adequate hot water made them more comfortable. The invention of what would be called 'the weekend' made them attractive places to spend the time between Saturday and Monday. The creation or growth in popularity of half-a-dozen pastimes (croquet, lawn tennis, billiards, motor-car and carriage driving, charades and amateur dramatics), added to the traditional pursuits of hunting, shooting and fishing, provided a wealth of amusements for the leisured classes. The invention of the gramophone meant that music was available, for dancing or merely for listening to, at any time of the day or night that one desired and that other guests would put up with. The country house was also, of course, an important setting for flirtation and for amorous affairs. It provided an enclosed world filled with pleasure and relaxation.

And, of course, many of these country dwellings were strikingly beautiful. Britain's increase in wealth over the nineteenth century meant that far more people could afford to live in country houses. Since there were not enough to go round, or because many of them were too out of date and uncomfortable to live in, new ones had to be built, and the result was that the Edwardian era became a golden age for British rural architecture. The Arts and Crafts Movement, an aesthetic reaction against the age of the machine, affected everything from the decoration of lampshades to the architectural style of private mansions and public buildings. It looked back to traditional methods of manufacture. The result was that country houses were no longer derivative of Classical architecture but drew from the vernacular, incorporating elements that were imaginative, witty, quirky, genuinely interesting. Though the houses were new their character derived from English buildings of the past, so that they would look as though they had always been there. The major figure in this architectural revolution, Sir Edwin Lutyens, created houses such as Goddards and Munstead Wood in Surrey that would still be admired more than a century later and would never go out of fashion. North of the border, his contemporary Sir Robert Lorimer created a style that, though similar, blended with the traditional architecture of Scotland. These houses later became national monuments, treasured because they capture the essence, the epitome, of a self-confident era that had no idea it was about to end.

By no means every family that occupied a country house actually owned it, of course. It was perfectly easy to rent one, filled with the portraits and ancestral clutter of others who perhaps could no longer afford to stay there. Though some tenants rented houses to live in all the year round, and those that were within convenient reach of London might be used for entertaining, it was more common to lease for a season a house or estate that came with specific sporting facilities – some in Hampshire were much in demand for their accompanying rights to fish on the River Test, for instance. Others, in northern England or the Scottish Highlands, had desirable rough-shooting in the surrounding woods, fields and moors. Amid the pastures of Leicestershire, houses were sought after from autumn to spring for their proximity to famous hunts. In Maidenhead on the Thames this notion of short seasonal renting was taken to extremes, for it was the 'only place to be seen' among members of Society on a single weekend every year. This was 'Ascot Sunday', the day following the races at nearby Ascot at the beginning of June. Once that had passed, the riverbanks rapidly emptied.

If you were a female inhabitant or guest at one of these houses, you had comparative freedom. Though you still left the gentlemen after dinner to their port and cigars, you would be able to dress less restrictively than your predecessors had done while outdoors, and as well as riding and following hounds you could bicycle or even play golf, since these were now considered acceptable pursuits for a woman. You might even, if you are sufficiently daring, ask to go out in the motor car and drive some distance yourself. There seems to have been a great deal less dreary sitting around than was previously the case.

Or was there? Social historian Gordon Winter commented in his book *The Golden Years* on country-house life during this heyday from another perspective: 'Somehow life at the top of the [income] bracket seems to have become unutterably boring. The social columns of the papers described the same people going through the same ritual year after year simply because it was thought to be the right thing to do. If overeating is a sign of boredom, these people excelled at it.' Whatever the pleasures available, it was true that they could be followed only in accordance with a rigid, unyielding set of conventions. It may have been a glittering era, but on reflection was not perhaps one in which it would have been an unmitigated pleasure to live.

Besides the leisured inhabitants of the world upstairs, there were of course the well-drilled and hard-working population of below stairs: the servants. Those who strove to make these houses and their surrounding estates function smoothly were sometimes career servants who would work anywhere, and sometimes retainers whose families had served there for generations. Both categories may well have felt a sense of belonging to the house and the family that employed them. They would also have had the constant companionship of other people like themselves, similar in background and experience, in hopes and dreams. The prospect, however distant, of foreign travel or of taking part in lavish entertainments and of being at close quarters to the wealthy and the famous and the glamorous – these things would all have been incentives to those who were in any case 'bettering' their lot by being in service. Such people were still available in sufficient numbers to keep the great country houses running in the years up to 1914, although in smaller, less affluent households there was a serious shortage by the end of the nineteenth century.

We must not, of course, imagine that these places were idyllic, or even easy, to work in. The problems of maintaining them would have been commensurate with their size and complexity. It was sometimes assumed by employers that to be surrounded by artistic treasures or great books would somehow make servants more refined and cultured, but the notion was derided by those whose only contact with beautiful objects was to clean them, often with not enough time to do so and in a state of constant anxiety in case they somehow caused damage. We should remember, as we admire the surviving treasures, that there was always a price paid by someone for maintaining their beauty and delicacy.

Interestingly, despite the fact that it was clearly hard work being a servant in a great house many people today, it seems, feel they would happily take on the burdens of service – at least until the novelty wore off. When in 2002 Channel 4 set out to re-create for a television series a fully functioning Edwardian country household, they received more applications from members of the public wanting to be servants than those seeking to be masters. It is also frequently the case that country houses open to the public today find that the most popular features with visitors are the re-created 'working' rooms – the kitchen, laundry or scullery – often featuring realistic mannequins dressed in old uniforms or livery.

Although there are still large houses lived in by wealthy families who need looking after, a British domestic servant is in fact a rarity today. The majority of those engaged as household staff are foreign nationals. Outside the Royal Household, little now remains of the hierarchical world of 'below stairs', a place that could, with its colourful liveries and arcane titles, be more structured and snobbish than its upstairs counterpart. It is a world that has largely vanished, thanks to rising costs, punitive taxation, a mass of labour-saving machines and an overwhelming general disinclination to pursue what is seen as menial work. Now safely consigned to the past, it is more of an escapist fantasy than an actual work prospect – but one that millions throughout the world continue to enjoy contemplating.

# 2

# THE PEOPLE AND THEIR HOUSES

'Oh! but the hideousness of everything, the showiness!
The sense of lavish wealth thrust up your nose! The
coarse mouldings, the heavy gilding always in the wrong
place, the colour of the silk hangings! Eye hath not seen
nor pen can write the ghastly coarseness of the sight!'
Lady Frances Balfour, describing the Rothschilds'
Halton House

The lifestyle enjoyed by the wealthy in the opening years
of the twentieth century had taken many generations to
create. The houses, like the tastes and pleasures of those
who occupied them, evolved over a lengthy period of
time. To appreciate what the Edwardians perfected, it is
worth considering what the country house was and how
it developed between the Middle Ages and the reign of
Edward VII.

There are several vintages of British aristocracy. The

oldest families are those descended from the soldiers who came to the British Isles with William the Conqueror, Duke of Normandy. He distributed the lands taken from the defeated Saxons among his followers, who in return owed him feudal allegiance – they were obliged to support him by raising troops in the event of war or emergency. Originally the Normans took control only of England; they were later to colonize Ireland, and to extend their influence far into Scotland. It is these members of the aristocracy, descended originally from Vikings who had settled in Normandy and then crossed the Channel with the Conqueror, who form the oldest stratum of the titled upper class.

Other families rose to prominence over the subsequent centuries, but the next sizeable intake into the landowning class took place during the English Reformation of the 1530s–40s. The Church had been – after the Crown – the biggest landowner in England. King Henry VIII, upon breaking from Rome, confiscated this land and thus vastly enriched himself. He sold on much of it to his wealthier subjects, who were eager for the prestige land ownership conferred. The King and his Protestant successors, Elizabeth I and James I, duly awarded titles to their favourites and thus launched a number of new aristocratic dynasties. Perhaps the greatest of these was the Cecil family, created Earls of Salisbury for their administrative service. Their country seat, Hatfield House in Hertfordshire, has remained a family possession ever since. An archetype of Jacobean brick architecture, it was built between 1608 and 1611, and is one of the best-known and most characteristic of early English country houses.

The third mass recruitment into the titled and land-owning aristocracy came towards the end of the nineteenth century. Wealth, and therefore power, had shifted decisively by that time from the old aristocracy to the new captains of commerce and industry. They wanted all the trappings that usually accompanied power, and increasingly governments instead of monarchs proposed such men for peerages or knighthoods. It is difficult perhaps for others to appreciate the extent to which the ownership of a country house has dominated the ambitions of talented men since there were first such places. The importance of the country villa in antiquity is well documented in the writings of, for instance, Horace (65–8 BC) and Pliny the Younger (c.61–112). The nineteenth-century newly rich bought land – and often houses – from the older cash-strapped aristocracy, or they built their own homes and continued the way of life traditional to country estates. There were so many such landowners in the last quarter of the century and the beginning of the next that they formed a distinct sub-class, leaving an indelible mark upon both the British landscape and British society through the houses they built and the bloodlines they revived.

Between 1850 and 1880, however, the British economy was booming. Gross National Product doubled in that time. Low taxation, low inflation, rising wages, booming markets both domestic and foreign, improving infrastructure in transport, largely unregulated markets, and a 25 per cent increase in population, all tipped the balance decisively in favour of the business elite at the expense of the traditional landowning aristocracy. Yet the ownership of land was still the thing to which both old and new rich aspired. It had been seen as the safest commodity, solid and eternal (as well as exclusive because its availability was limited), the antithesis of stocks and shares that went up and down in value. Between 1875 and 1897, however, the cost of agricultural land fell by more than half, going from £54 an acre to a mere £19. Nevertheless it kept an almost mystic hold on the imagination of the old and new rich, as a symbol of solidity, permanence and authority.

Of the three things that characterized the ruling elite – money, land and title – those who had the first seemed almost inevitably to want the others. Titles were, by the early twentieth century, becoming relatively easy to obtain in any case, for King Edward VII, friend of so many *arriviste* plutocrats, raised no objection to ennobling them, and in fact created four times as many baronets as his mother had done. During the premiership of Lloyd George, titles would even be sold semi-openly by the Government. Julius Drewe of Castle Drogo was offered one, but considered it too expensive at £100,000.

The oldest families naturally lived in castles. Their power originally depended on military might as much as on possession of land because under their feudal obligation they had to impose the king's authority on the surrounding area. In an era of instability – and in England this lasted from the Norman Conquest to the late seventeenth century – it was necessary to have physical protection from your enemies. Some families still dwell within the original defensive fortifications thrown up by their forebears. To cite one example: the Percy family, Earls and then Dukes of Northumberland, have lived at Alnwick Castle since they bought it in

November 1309 from the Bishop of Durham. (They still have the deed of sale!) Set in a strategic position commanding the Northumbrian countryside, the castle provided vital protection against attack from marauding Scots, and remained a military outpost for many centuries. It still looks like one, with serviceable, battlemented walls and towers that would withstand considerable punishment. Their home is, after Windsor, the largest still-inhabited castle in Britain.

The ramparts remain, of course, as a picturesque reminder of the Castle's former strategic importance, but they were remodelled to add beauty and further quaintness by Robert Adam in the eighteenth century. The surrounding meadows were once forested for hunting, but were cleared and replanted by the great Capability Brown (1716–1783) to make a landscape that, though it is working agricultural land, looks as contrived as it in fact is. His work is to be found as far away as Russia (Munich still has an English garden). Inside, the building has naturally been modernized in keeping with domestic rather than defensive use. Its crude medieval might was early on counterbalanced by lavish State Apartments and elegant Georgian plasterwork. The Percys have not (like the Dukes of Rutland at their home in Belvoir Castle in Leicestershire) replaced the medieval fortress with a more comfortable, later version of a Gothic castle. They did not need to make such sweeping changes to their ancestral home because they had others – two major houses in and near London (their property at Syon in Middlesex was designed by the Adam brothers in the 1770s). Alnwick Castle, meanwhile, has become known throughout the world as a location for films, which not only helps publicize it to potential visitors but brings in useful extra revenue. Of the eight films that have to date been made in the grounds, the most well-known must be *Harry Potter and the Philosopher's Stone* (2001) and its sequel *Harry Potter and the Chamber of Secrets* (2002), where the castle features as the exterior of Hogwarts School. New life for an ancient house.

The Berkeleys live in Gloucestershire. They have sometimes been titled – they were Earls of Berkeley – and sometimes not. Their Norman ancestor, Roger de Berkeley, died in 1193, and his descendants still live in the castle he built, with its circular keep and outer courtyard, overlooking the surrounding meadows. This family home, like Alnwick Castle, looks as if it could still withstand a siege, and many of its interiors are plain and feudal in appearance. It is easy to imagine this house as the setting for a medieval battle, but more difficult to picture an Edwardian ball going on there.

Country houses, in other words, are extremely varied in terms of size, appearance, facilities, sumptuousness. They may have been demolished and rebuilt, or altered out of recognition, or left more or less as they were originally built. Changes depend on the family's wealth or upon its sense of fashion. Some – the socially or politically ambitious – wished to be at the forefront of current taste while others, devoted to their land rather than to prestige, allowed their homes to remain unaltered.

Blair Castle is in Scotland, set in Perthshire against the backdrop of the Grampian Mountains. It has been the home of the Earls, later the Dukes, of Atholl since the

fifteenth century, though the oldest part of the building
dates from 1269. Though large, undoubtedly imposing
and conspicuous – its whitewashed walls are visible for
miles against the dark, pine-covered hills – it is obvious
at a glance that it was not planned but has evolved over
the centuries from a much smaller structure. It has
considerable vernacular charm but, despite having been
extensively remodelled in the eighteenth century, it lacks
the decorative touches so beloved of the Georgians.
There are no Grecian-style columns, no balustrades, no
splendid pediments, no statuary. It looks grimly defensive rather than built for pleasure or to show off art
collections. It began as a fortress and remained one until
the eighteenth century. Indeed in one of those quirks of
history that make British country houses so much fun to
examine, the Dukes are entitled to raise and maintain the
only private army in Britain. The Atholl Highlanders, a
splendidly kilted unit that parades in the Duke's tartan,
armed with archaic weaponry, is the last remnant of the
bands of armed followers that were, until relatively
recently, a necessity for all Highland chieftains. Again,
this house is not short of historical romance, but it would
not fit with the image of Victorian or Edwardian luxury
that so often comes to mind when we imagine the world
of the country house. Its interiors, it must be said in
fairness, are very imposing. The dining room is a
showpiece of the plasterer's art, and the sporting facilities
– the fishing, shooting and stalking so dear to the hearts
of the upper class – are magnificent. It is undeniably a
great house, but somehow looks too intimate to be a
ducal estate.

The advent of the Tudor dynasty, which came to

power in the person of Henry VII in 1485, brought to an end the decades of strife that had ravaged England through the fifteenth century. Houses built after that date gradually came to look less like fortresses and more like homes. There was a new symmetry in their outline; there were windows on the ground floor. In the sixteenth century, throughout the reigns of Henry VIII, Edward VI, Mary I and Elizabeth I, the country went through religious convulsions that amounted to a revolution, but this did not involve – as it did on the Continent – actual warfare. England's architecture continued its peaceful development. A house like Hardwick Hall in Derbyshire (1565), for instance, not only displays no defensive features but boasts considerable variety of decoration, not least in the repeated motif of the initials 'ES' on its roof balustrade, proclaiming its owner to be Elizabeth Hardwick, Countess of Shrewsbury (more commonly known as Bess of Hardwick). It is difficult to imagine such fripperies being added even to a grand house a generation or two earlier.

After Henry VIII's break from Rome, those men who were wealthy enough to buy monastic lands from the king very often acquired a title to go with them. An entire new class of aristocrats emerged. The names of their family seats often betray their architectural origins: the Dukes of Bedford live at Woburn Abbey, for instance; the Byron family, to which the poet belonged, lived at Newstead Abbey; Sir Henry Fox-Talbot, the pioneer of photography, lived at Lacock Abbey. Of these three houses, one – Woburn – has been rebuilt as a Palladian mansion that bears no resemblance to a monastery. The other two, probably because the families were not wealthy enough to demolish and rebuild, are the original monastic buildings and still look, from the outside at least, much as they did before the Reformation. Both of them still have cloisters. In the case of Byron, his ancestral home (which he had eventually to sell to pay off his debts) provided the perfect setting of Gothic romance for a man who revelled in the dissolute reputation that he had.

One of the grandest country houses ever built in England was Hampton Court, sited on the Thames some miles south-west of London. It was created for Cardinal Thomas Wolsey (1474–1530), Archbishop, Chancellor, and national administrator for the young King Henry VIII, between 1517 and 1520. The size of a Cambridge college and, with its chapel and great hall and brick-paved courtyard, looking remarkably similar to one, like its creator it proved too ostentatious for the king's liking. Henry confiscated it when Wolsey fell from grace and, considerably added to in a later era, it has been a royal palace ever since. Its original core represents several things. First, it shows a distinctive type of architecture that is instantly recognizable as both English and Tudor, a style that first became established because of this building, though paradoxically a number of craftsmen were imported from other countries to help create it. Secondly, it was a triumph of domestic architecture, showing what glories could be created if one's budget were large enough. Wolsey was the richest man in England after the monarch; he need spare no expense in purchasing land and materials, or in hiring the skills of those who used them. He thought on a grand scale, as can be seen from his other great surviving building project: Christ Church, Oxford. Hampton Court is the prototype for the purpose-built country house.

It was in the sixteenth century that architects first began creating country houses from scratch, in the grand manner, rather than adapting existing military or religious buildings into private dwellings, and it would be a further hundred years before such a practice fully got into its stride. The first Baroque house in England was Chatsworth in Derbyshire, built for the Duke of Devonshire by William Talman from 1687–96, and still lived in by the Devonshires today. Talman was rapidly eclipsed by another, untrained but highly gifted, architect, Sir John Vanbrugh (1664–1726). He was a surprisingly versatile man who not only created great houses despite his complete lack of architectural training (he collaborated with the great Nicholas Hawksmoor, 1661–1736, who could provide the necessary professional skills), but also earned an honourable place in the canon of English literature by writing comedies that are still performed, *The Relapse* and *The Provok'd Wife* being the most well-known. He had travelled widely, to both India and the Continent. Imprisoned for more than four years in Paris, he came to know and admire French architecture and was influenced by such buildings as the Louvre and the Château Fortress of Vincennes. He also educated himself in English architecture by making a tour of many of the grandest existing country seats.

A man of winning charm and ready wit, Vanbrugh won the friendship, and thus the patronage, of several extremely powerful men. In particular his membership of the Whig 'Kit-Cat Club' brought him into contact with the 3rd Earl of Carlisle (1669–1738) whom he persuaded to employ him as builder in the building of Castle Howard, the Earl's seat in Yorkshire. Work there began in 1699, as soon as Vanbrugh had returned from his inspirational tour.

The result was highly impressive. Castle Howard became the most continental-looking house in Britain, a Baroque masterpiece that was, however, very English in its comparative subtlety and understatement. The same was said, incidentally, of Christopher Wren's rebuilt St Paul's Cathedral, a project that was its near contemporary (1675–1708). It was not the cathedral but the great house, however, that was to make the Baroque suddenly fashionable in England. Castle Howard was undeniably grand, if less flamboyant than its counterparts in Europe. The house had a domed central block to contain the family's rooms for living and receiving in, as well as for displaying their notable collections of paintings, antiquities and bronzes. This central building was flanked by two matching wings housing the more prosaic elements of life – the servants' quarters, laundry and stables.

Lord Stanhope, observing Castle Howard from a distance in its setting of parkland embellished with the works of man and nature – gazebos, lawns, stands of trees – was deeply impressed by the 'temples on high places, worthy of being each a metropolis of the Druids ... the noblest lawn in the world fenced by half the horizon, and a mausoleum that would tempt one to be buried alive. I have seen gigantic palaces before, but never a sublime one.'

Castle Howard gave Vanbrugh such pre-eminence that, only five years after starting on the Yorkshire house, he was granted the most prestigious architectural commission in the land. Blenheim Palace was to be built by the nation in thanks to John Churchill, 1st Duke of Marlborough. Churchill was a military commander who had defeated the mighty forces of King Louis XIV at the Bavarian village of Blindheim (anglicized to Blenheim). The Government was to bear the cost, and the house was to be a national war memorial as well as a family home. The former function, in fact, was to become the more important, and Blenheim would never be a comfortable place in which to live. The Duke's wife Sarah, a woman of formidable personality, disliked Vanbrugh's design from the beginning for that precise reason, and their quarrels would eventually lead him to resign before the project was completed.

The Duchess had wanted Sir Christopher Wren to undertake the work, but it was the Queen and the Government, not Sarah herself, who decided how big the house should be. Though she was not paying for it, the Duchess objected to the soaring cost and to the architect's extravagance. (Her husband, equally tight-fisted, was said never to dot his 'i's when writing, as a way of saving ink.) After quarrelling with the Queen and falling from favour, the Duchess and her husband went to live abroad, returning to England only after Queen Anne's death. The rift meant that the sovereign ceased to pay for work on Blenheim, and it must therefore be completed at the Marlboroughs' own expense. Costs were immediately cut, new – and allegedly less skilled – workmen were employed, and after a major argument Vanbrugh walked off site and abandoned the project, which had to be finished by his colleague Hawksmoor.

The Duchess did not forgive him, and when in 1725 he attempted to visit Blenheim, paying like any other member of the public, he was forbidden to enter even the grounds, let alone the house.

Blenheim became the largest non-royal residence in Britain. It looms from a distance out of its parkland like a great golden citadel. It has been described, both at the time and since, as looking more like a fortress – or indeed a fortified city – than a country house. In the manner of Castle Howard it comprises a central block for the family with, rather than wings that sweep into the distance, two rectangular blocks for the servants and their activities, built around courtyards. There is another very imposing entrance courtyard that visitors only see after they have passed through a massive stone triumphal arch. The scale of the house is so massive that anyone reaching it must feel diminished. It is a memorial not to a great family but to one man. The focus within the grounds is the column from which the 1st Duke's statue looks down on his domain, and even in the chapel where he is buried, the interior is dominated not by religious emblems or by statues of saints but by another carved stone likeness of him. Blenheim, the apotheosis of Baroque architecture in Britain, was the biggest, the grandest, the most overwhelming country house in English history.

The homes given to other, later great commanders – for this became the traditional reward for military valour – have never been so overwhelming. Over a century after Vanbrugh worked on Blenheim, the Duke of Wellington was given the house of Stratfield Saye. Nelson, though killed in his moment of triumph, had already been given

Merton Place on the outskirts of London. Though grand enough to house a member of the aristocracy, neither was as glaringly, deliberately awe-inspiring as Blenheim. Though admired by some, the house did not provide a popular model to be followed by other architects or landowners.

One person who saw it early on was Voltaire. As a Frenchman he might perhaps have been expected to dislike its bombastic triumphalism. His reaction was instead one of amusement. 'What a great heap of stone,' he commented, 'without charm or taste.' It was also remarked at the time that the house – both inside and out – resembled a stage set, and this may not have been coincidental, given the architect's other occupation. It does indeed seem like a film set, and has been used as one: it featured as the Castle of Elsinore in Kenneth Branagh's production of *Hamlet* (1996). The present Duke of Marlborough enjoyed the experience so much that he took part in the film himself.

Vanbrugh's third and final design was also created for a military hero. Seaton Delaval in Northumberland is considerably smaller than Blenheim, as befits a more modest victory. It was begun in 1718 for Admiral George Delaval. Once again it resembles a fortress, though this time a more intimate family dwelling than a major defensive work. Its style is rather more austere, as perhaps befits a house set in the barer landscape of north-east England, though ironically it owes more to European influences – it borrows heavily from Palladio's Villa Foscari – than do Vanbrugh's other designs.

One thing that makes British country houses such a pleasure to study or to visit is the sense of humour, playfulness and sheer daftness that is often displayed by their owners and builders. This is not an area in which they can claim to be unique, for similar examples abound throughout Europe and the world. The site of the Arc de Triomphe in Paris was at one time destined to be occupied by a giant statue of an elephant, which visitors could climb, and the gardens of Versailles and Tivoli and Peterhof contain trick fountains that squirt the unwary. Yet among the British upper class there is a long tradition of eccentricity, and this has sometimes found expression in their houses.

'The Pineapple' is in Scotland, near the town of Falkirk. It is on an estate formerly owned by an aristocratic family: the Murrays, Earls of Dunmore. In 1761 they had a hothouse built in the Palladian style on the edge of a walled garden. It was a long structure on two storeys, the lower of which was for the growing of the exotic fruit in a tropical climate provided by furnaces and air-ducts. The floor above was for the accommodation of the gardeners. When the 4th Earl, who served as Governor of New York until the outbreak of the American Revolution, returned to Scotland he commissioned an addition – a stone pineapple some 46 feet tall, with a room inside that would form a cupola and act as a summerhouse. No one is entirely sure who designed and built it, though opinion favours Sir William Chambers, an architect who contributed much to the beauty both of Scottish country houses and to the New Town of Edinburgh. The Pineapple is perfect in its botanical detail – as is to be expected, when specimens of the fruit were growing only feet away in the hothouse beneath. It is built of the same limestone as the rest of the building, and sits like a crown over the entrance arch, perfectly symmetrical with the rest of the building, and looking as if it had always been intended to be there. It is so cleverly contrived that water cannot collect anywhere on the segmented surface or among the leaves, to form ice and thus crack the stone in cold weather. One of the most splendidly exotic buildings in Europe, the Pineapple is a tribute both to the man who commissioned it and to the one who created it. It now belongs to the National Trust for Scotland but can be rented by members of the public as a holiday home (they stay in the gardeners' cottages to either side of the actual fruit).

Because it has always been a trading nation, Britain has for centuries been open to influences from all parts of the world. It is commonplace in British country houses to find a mix of styles recalling the travels of a past owner, who brought back drawings, plans or even stonework and architectural features to beautify his family home. This was especially the case during the heyday of the Grand Tour (c.1660–1840s), when young aristocrats, after finishing their studies at school or university, were sent on a circular tour of the European continent to make what they could of the treasures of antiquity. From Paris they travelled to Rome, then to Naples and Herculaneum to view the ruins of Pompeii. They returned via Germany and the Low Countries. In an age of difficult and expensive travel this was a once-in-a-lifetime look at the world before they settled down, to run their estate or sit in Parliament. It was not only an education but a shopping trip, for they brought home antiquities by the shipload. (Literally, in some cases. If a young man had bought some large and cumbersome statuary he might be able, through parental influence or the good offices of a British Consul, to have it conveyed by any naval vessel conveniently in port.)

The influence of these journeys is everywhere to be seen in the 'stately homes of England'. It is visible, for instance, in the entrance hall at Holkham Hall in Norfolk which, with its marble floors, alabaster columns and coffered ceiling, was modelled on the Pantheon in Rome. The paintings that decorate many houses also bear witness to the Grand Tour. Canvases by Pompeo Batoni (1708–87), showing fashionably dressed young men lounging against ancient statuary, are owned by a number of aristocratic British families. Even more well known are the Venetian views of Antonio Canal (Canaletto, 1731–85). These elegant paintings helped to form an idealized image of Italy for generations of Britons.

The Grand Tour, as a significant feature of aristocratic education, was brought to an end by the outbreak of the French Revolution and the subsequent war in which France and the United Kingdom fought on opposite sides. The conflict would last until the defeat of Napoleon in 1815 and would close the Continent of Europe to British travellers for a generation. Without the chance to look at foreign scenery, Englishmen were obliged to admire their own instead. The wilder corners of the British Isles had to substitute: Snowdonia for the Apennines, Bath or Edinburgh for Paris or Vienna. It helped Englishmen to realize that there were romantic landscapes to be seen in their own realm and to reawaken interest, and even pride, in what they had.

For nearly three and a half centuries Britain was involved with the Indian subcontinent, commercially, militarily and administratively. Hundreds of thousands of men served with the East India Company between 1599 and 1857, and many of them returned home with sizeable fortunes. One of these, Colonel John Cockerell, purchased the estate of Sezincote near Moreton-in-Marsh in Gloucestershire from the Earl of Guildford in 1795, and commissioned one of his brothers, Samuel Pepys Cockerell, to build him a house that would evoke the architectural and decorative style of India.

Samuel was a trained architect who had also served in the East, as Surveyor to the East India Company. He had already built a nearby house for another Indian 'nabob', Warren Hastings. At Sezincote, which was completed in 1810, he created a building that is still admired. It has a central block crowned by a Mughal dome and flanked by spindly minarets, and there is a single, sweeping wing that houses an orangery. The gardens were laid out in a Persian manner with many pools, though in the damp English climate this did not have the same luxuriant effect as in the Middle East. Sezincote is a jewel, a bastardized fragment of the Mughal world transported to a setting that is completely alien and unsympathetic, yet somehow it works. The house was to become the model for the famous Brighton Pavilion.

The Prince of Wales (later George IV) maintained a large home – Carlton House – in London, but wished to own a residence far enough from the capital to pursue his personal life in private, having secretly married a Roman Catholic. Brighton, a town on the Sussex coast some sixty miles south of London, was then becoming established as a fashionable summer resort under the patronage of his uncle, the Duke of Cumberland. In 1786 the Prince rented, and then bought, a farmhouse in the town, and the following year commissioned the architect Henry Holland to extend and beautify it. Holland would be the first of three architects to remodel a building that continued growing both in size and ornamentation as the prince became more and more committed to it. The farmhouse came to form one wing that was connected to a large rotunda that contained public rooms. A conservatory and a larger dining room were added in renovations in 1801–2, and at the same time a huge riding school was built on the other side of the garden.

A third round of expansion took place between 1815–22, this time under the direction of John Nash, who was later to build Buckingham Palace. The exteriors of Brighton Pavilion, as it became known after initially being named the Marine Pavilion, were a riot of Indian domes, cupolas, minarets. The interiors, though these also boast some Indian influence, were Chinese in style, echoing the fashion for 'Chinoiserie' that had dominated Europe in the eighteenth century. Brighton Pavilion was a structure entirely alien to its English setting, whimsy on a huge scale, a royal residence of such eccentricity that its equal would not be seen until the creations of King Ludwig II of Bavaria half a century later. The house passed eventually to the Prince's heir, Queen Victoria, who did not like it (it was far too close to the public streets to offer any privacy) and created her own summer home on the Isle of Wight. It was bought from the Crown by the town of Brighton and used for public events, but during the Great War in the following century, in a highly ironic twist of fate, was converted into a hospital for . . . Indian soldiers.

The most ambitious country house in Britain, as well as by far the most eccentric, took shape amid the Wiltshire countryside between 1796 and 1813. Fonthill Abbey was the home of William Beckford (1760–1844). To describe him as wealthy would be a considerable understatement. Indeed he was described as 'the richest commoner in England'. At the age of ten he inherited a fortune derived from West Indian sugar plantations that would be the equivalent of more than £100 million today, and thus grew up unable to remember a time when he could not gratify any wish. He was, however, an unusual character with few friends. Suspected of homosexuality and the victim of what might now be termed a 'hate campaign', he was not regarded as acceptable by English Society and spent some years travelling on the Continent, absorbing its history and architecture. He was the author of a book, begun when he was twenty-one, called *Vathek* – one of the 'Gothic novels' in vogue in his lifetime – and this has given him a modest renown in English literature.

An admirer of the Gothic Revival architecture that had been used to such effect at Sir Horace Walpole's Strawberry Hill and which was to remain in fashion for a century, Beckford too wanted to live in a medieval fantasy. Though he could probably have found a Tudor country house of the Lacock Abbey sort – a converted monastic building – to adapt to his taste, he did not do so. He could with equal ease have rebuilt any number of genuine, pre-Reformation ecclesiastical ruins and made himself a home from them. He could have remodelled the family house he inherited – Fonthill Splendens. Instead he chose to build himself a medieval-style abbey, on a scale bigger than Glastonbury or Bury St Edmunds, from the ground up. He also wanted it built fast.

Though Beckford was in a tearing hurry to have it finished, the architect he employed, Thomas Wyatt, was notoriously slow and inefficient, wasting time to the extent that his projects might be whole years behind schedule, and frequently failing to turn up for meetings with his patrons or clients. During his periodic absences Beckford simply took over supervision of the work. The plan called for a massive structure that was not – like a real monastery – built around a cloister or a series of courtyards, but instead formed a cruciform shape with four long wings. These converged on a central octagonal space that was to be topped with a tower 300 feet high. Beckford was so committed to the project that he employed 500 workmen and had them organized into shifts that worked round the clock. When these proved insufficient he almost doubled their numbers by bringing in another 450, enticing them away from Windsor Castle where they had been working for the King. His tactic was simple – he promised them a more generous beer ration!

Like many later houses in the nineteenth century, when grand new homes would be thick upon the ground, Fonthill was deliberately designed to look as if it had stood for centuries by incorporating different architectural styles, suggesting changing fashions and the work of one generation overlaying or altering that of the last.

Wyatt had suggested for the central tower a material called 'compo cement' – timber to which wet cement was applied as a kind of stucco. This was not suitable for a structure so tall or so massive, and the tower collapsed.

It was simply rebuilt, six years later, but this too fell down. Beckford, whose enthusiasm for the building seemingly could not be dented even by disasters on this scale, ordered it to be rebuilt immediately. This took a further seven years, but this time stone was used and the tower stayed up – until 1825, when it collapsed for the third and final time. Here was an intriguing instance of history repeating itself. As readers of William Golding's novel *The Spire* will know, medieval cathedral builders had faced the constant danger that ambitiously tall towers would not stand up. They had understood far less about structural engineering, and had had to proceed by trial and error. If Fonthill had been a genuine medieval abbey, it might well have suffered the collapse of its central tower. For this to happen so many centuries later implied that construction techniques had not advanced greatly over the intervening years, but then no tower of this height had been attempted by builders of any era.

The house was finished, give or take the fine details, in 1813. As a largely friendless man, Beckford did not inaugurate it with a public celebration. He did not feast his neighbours, or invite royalty or aristocracy to stay. He lived there alone, occupying only a few of the numerous rooms, though his household staff would have filled the servants' quarters. He dined alone, though he wished twelve meals to be prepared and sent in on each occasion, he chose one and the rest were returned. He hosted visitors only once; Lord Nelson and his mistress Lady Hamilton were his guests. In that year Nelson, having defeated Napoleon at the Battle of the Nile and thus put an end to French control of Egypt (Britain feared this would threaten the Indian Empire), was the greatest celebrity – and therefore presumably the most sought-after dinner guest – in the land. Thus Beckford's only venture into hospitality at least netted him the country's biggest celebrity. One winter he announced that he would not eat Christmas dinner unless it had been prepared in the new kitchens he had ordered to be built. His workmen rushed the job – never a sensible thing to do, especially when dealing with building on this scale – and the dinner was duly ready in time, though the kitchens fell down as soon as he had finished the meal.

Beckford remained at Fonthill until 1822. His tenure ended not because of falling masonry but because he had to sell. In that year he was involved in a legal dispute over property in Jamaica, and was obliged to dispose of both his house and its contents. Though it might have been seen as a colossal white elephant – a single man's dream that would not appeal to anyone else – he found a buyer in John Farquhar, an extremely wealthy maker of ammunition, who paid the colossal sum of £330,000 for the house. He was not getting much of a bargain. Three years later the central tower fell down again, wrecking one of the wings. The house was soon abandoned, and most of it demolished. Well before the death of its builder, Fonthill was a pile of rubble and dubbed 'Beckford's folly'. Its sheer scale made it too impractical to live in or to maintain. It is probably something of a mercy that it fell down. Though parts of it still exist, the cost of upkeep for the complete building would no doubt have proved ruinous.

Beckford's grand project in a sense heralded the arrival of a new era. Never in Britain's history would so many great houses be built as in the nineteenth century. Never had such an influx of newcomers been able to afford the symbols, and the pleasures, of immense wealth. The *nouveau riche* far outnumbered those already in possession of property and land. They could have swamped the existing landowning class, changed it beyond recognition, remade all the rules. Yet they did not. The vast shift of wealth towards the middle class was no revolution. It did not see a redefining of social norms as the values of one class were replaced by those of another, nor any widening of the interests of the upper class. What happened instead was that the new arrivals effectively attached themselves to the way of life already in existence, and followed – often with slavish devotion – the behaviour and habits of those already at the top.

With polite society travelling between London, Bath, Brighton and other centres of entertainment, country houses were seen as useful places in which to break a journey, and at the appropriate times of year large numbers of people did so. If you were well dressed enough to look like a member of 'polite' circles, you might expect to arrive at any house and be shown around it.

Calling at, and being shown around houses, whether they were occupied at the time by their owners or not, became an established pleasure of the polite tourist. The visit by Jane Austen's Elizabeth Bennet to the home of Mr Darcy, with the customary tour conducted by the housekeeper (for whom the tips given by such callers would be an important source of income), is a well-known literary instance of this. From the 1790s, when war against the French closed the European continent to

English travellers and ruled out the Grand Tour, houses that echoed the architectural glories of Greece and Rome, and contained archaeological and artistic relics of them, became an important source of education for those who could no longer see the originals. The country house, which in previous ages had been largely a place from which to run the estate or sit out the winter (it was the town house in which collections were displayed and much polite entertaining done), now became a place to visit on its own account. At the same time, the Agricultural Revolution had made farming more profitable and efficient. Not only were up-to-date, well-run estates instructive and pleasurable to visit, they were also places that absorbed the energies and roused the passionate enthusiasm of their owners.

With fast coaches and good roads, the age of country-house visiting had properly arrived, and these houses adapted to accommodate house parties. From the 1760s onward the bell-pull – a system that linked every room upstairs to the servants' wing or hall – meant that maids and footmen could be summoned from distant quarters and need no longer hang about the corridors (in many houses the small wooden chairs they used, decorated with the family coat of arms, can still be seen), waiting to be called upon. The servants' bell board made it possible to see at a glance in which room of the house they were required, but the bells went on ringing for up to ten minutes to encourage the slow or unwilling! By the latter decades of the eighteenth century a system of bells connected by a rope was commonplace in country houses, and the system became more sophisticated over the following century.

The house party was a largely informal affair. Groups of people, both old friends and new acquaintances, stayed together in a house for a matter of days or weeks or even months. Activities were unstructured, apart from meeting for meals and during sporting expeditions, so that guests were left much of the time to do as they liked. It was not considered necessary for everyone to participate in the same things. They could seek diversion alone or with any number of others. Above all they were free to be idle. The communal rooms of English country houses became places for relaxation, in which lounging was perfectly acceptable. A major aspect of them – and a prime preoccupation for many participants – was the chance they offered for courting: meeting and impressing members of the opposite sex, with a view to marriage. In these informal gatherings, in which people might be in each other's proximity for a matter of weeks, it was easily possible to find oneself conducting a romance. This lifestyle was, once again, captured by Miss Austen, who described not only the pleasures of this life of endless leisure but the boredom and backbiting that so often accompanied it. Nevertheless the house party, a product of the nineteenth century's opening years and, in keeping with the spirit of that time, a reaction against the formality of the previous century, became a British institution.

Because the gentry and aristocracy were spending more time in the country, the entertainments in these houses became bigger and grander. There was a distinct revival, at the end of the eighteenth century, in the practice of hosting large dinners for the local tenantry, to celebrate the usual family, local or national events. These were more than mere gestures of goodwill or charity. They served to demonstrate concern for the poor and thus to emphasize – in an era dominated by the French Revolution – that the English aristocracy were closer to their people and more aware of their needs than the haughty members of France's *Ancien Régime*. For the upper class, at the same time, the country house acted as a sort of extended club, to which anyone in polite society might, given an introduction, gain admission.

Facilities also became better. Running water had been available in country houses since the seventeenth century. Before the middle of the eighteenth it was possible to have this on all floors thanks to efficient pumping. Baths and water closets were widely used. By the late eighteenth century there were small baths for individuals (as opposed to a large plunge bath) and efficient lavatories. Joseph Bramah's water closet – if that can be taken as a general benchmark of comfort – was patented in 1778. They became ubiquitous in country houses after that date, though they were not, of course, installed for the servants' use. The latter would probably have continued the immemorial custom, formerly practised by all classes, of simply going down the garden to do their business ('going to pluck a rose' was a phrase then equivalent to 'powdering one's nose') – the results, of course, were useful as fertilizer. Lighting was, even by Jane Austen's time, becoming a matter of oil lamps rather than candles, though these in turn began to be supplanted by gas within her lifetime. Steam heating arrived in the early nineteenth century and crude radiators were used, as at Stratfield Saye where the Duke of Wellington installed them in the 1830s.

In spite of this, there was a curious reluctance to adopt all the technological advances that were now available. On the other side of Europe, William I of Prussia had been appalled when told that flush lavatories could now be installed in his palaces, and exclaimed: 'We're having none of that new-fangled nonsense around here!' The King also refused to have his own bathtub. Once a week he borrowed one from the hotel across the road. Though his is an extreme example, it illustrates the suspicion of both new technology and physical comfort that was characteristic of a certain northern European mindset.

The British in that era were intensely aware of their country's power, wealth and greatness. They feared that this could be diminished through the moral softening caused by wallowing in luxury. This was one reason for the preoccupation of the upper class with vigorous sports such as hunting, stalking and shooting. Although they might be waited upon hand and foot, they would earn their ease through exertion and by acquiring sporting prowess. The country houses which they visited or in which they lived had, by the early decades of the nineteenth century, such advanced plumbing, heating and lighting that they were the wonder – and the envy – of aristocracies throughout Europe, enjoying a level of comfort that was at least a generation, if not half a century, away for many more modest English homes. Yet as Mark Girouard has written in his seminal *Life in the English Country House*: 'In the next fifty years, advances in the available technology were not matched by equivalent advances in comfort. Luxury, to the Victorians, tended to be a suspect word.' It is clear that, whereas our own definition of a 'great house' would be based on the comfort it offers and the facilities it can boast, for the builders and occupiers of these places it was sheer magnificence that counted most.

No activity is more completely associated with the country house than foxhunting, despite the fact that pursuing this animal on horseback is equally common in Ireland, Europe, America and Australia. As with so many sports and games, it is the British who have formalised, codified and refined it, however.

The hunting of foxes with dogs by the English is first mentioned in 1534, though it would be more than a century before packs of hounds would be in regular use, and it would not be until the eighteenth century that specially bred animals would be seen. The great English hunts: the Quorn in Leicestershire (1696), the Pytchely in Northamptonshire (1750), the Beaufort in Gloucestershire (1682) gained renown throughout Britain and beyond. The Midlands, the region more or less in the centre of England and a place ironically associated with heavy industry, became the mecca for hunting, centred on the town of Melton Mowbray in Leicestershire. The landscape there – gentle hills and valleys given over to pasture – was ideal for the chase, and during the hunting season Melton played host to much of Society. Its streets were filled with horseboxes, grooms and men in 'pink' (the scarlet of the coats worn by huntsmen is correctly termed pink, perhaps in reference to the shirtmaker Thomas Pink, who made such garments). Ladies, who also hunted, wore not a coat but a collar in the livery of the hunt, and dressed otherwise in black.

A hunt was – as it still is – overseen by a Master of Foxhounds (MFH) who was the administrator as well as being in charge of the kennels. If he did not have time to do everything himself he might share the job and be a 'Joint-Master.' There was also a Huntsman, armed with a short, braying horn, who would control the hounds once the chase began. He would be assisted by 'whippers-in' or 'whips' who imposed order on the hounds and who have given their name to the parliamentary officials responsible for party discipline.

The hunt would meet at a prearranged place – the yard of a rural pub, or the lawn in front of a country house, to take a drink (a stirrup-cup) before setting off, and guests who wished to ride with it would at this point pay toward the costs. Then the hounds would set off, following the scent of any foxes they picked up, and the horsemen would follow. Naturally there might be more than one fox, so the pursuit could last for hours. The chase would cover many miles of countryside, testing the rider's skill with fences, hedges, streams, and this exercise would be regarded as compensation even if no fox were killed. The quarry might otherwise be caught and dismembered by the hounds, or disappear into the ground, in which case a hunt servant would bring terriers to dig it out. Its carcass was given to the hounds – their reward for hard work. The brush (tail) and the mask (face) might be taken as trophies by the members of the hunt. It was customary that new members be 'blooded' – smeared on the face by the Huntsman with blood from the fox, as a rite of passage. This was a very common childhood experience for members of the landed aristocracy.

Why did hunting reach such a level of social prestige in Britain, between the mid-Victorian age and the Second

World War? The British love horses, and this activity enabled both mount and rider not only to gain invigorating exercise but to experience excitement, tension, danger and great exhilaration. For a sedentary society, hunting was a release from the predictability of things, a chance for those whose lives contained little excitement – and perhaps little physical strain – to engage in a battle of wits with nature. The qualities needed by a medieval knight – courage and daring, skill in riding – were those found in a competent 'rider to hounds.' Cavalry officers were expected to hunt regularly because to do so sharpened their skills and trained them in assessing a landscape in which an enemy might hide. Men therefore engaged in hunting because it was manly. Women did so (sidesaddle of course!) because it offered them too an escape from the constraints of their class and its lifestyle. Their 'role model' – the most famous huntswoman of the nineteenth century and a regular visitor to the shires, was Elizabeth, Empress of Austria (1837-98). Possessed of great beauty and personal charm as well as being a highly-skilled horsewoman, she added even greater glamour to a sport that already carried more than a whiff of aristocracy.

Foxhunting was made illegal in Britain in 2005, at least partly because a sullen public disliked the notion of the rich conspicuously enjoying themselves. The law has proved difficult to enact, and legal challenges are still being mounted. In the meantime the hunts and the packs of hounds survive. They chase the fox but do not kill it, or they flush it out to be shot (which is legal), or they follow trails of scented rags. They retain the splendid liveries with their distinctive buttons, they still hold the annual hunt balls, and the social side of the sport continues. Though understandably associated with the upper class, hunting is surprisingly egalitarian. Many of those who assemble to ride, or to follow the hunt on foot, are farmers or countrymen or simply curious members of the public (the controversy of recent years has apparently led to an increase in membership of hunts). But not all packs have, in any case, been run by aristocrats. A highly successful one is the Banwen Miners' Hunt, established in 1963 by Welsh miners who deliberately wanted to make the sport available to members of the working class. Their hunt, like the others, is still going strong, and its patron is the Duke of Beaufort.

Shooting (largely the killing of game birds such as pheasant), the other field sport that is seen as peculiarly British, became popular for the same reason as hunting. It required skills, in this case precision, patience, nerve, perfect hand-and-eye. With the development, from the eighteenth century, of increasingly better shotguns, there was also the pleasure of using beautifully-designed equipment and the great English gunmakers – Purdey, and Holland and Holland – were seen as leading the world in this form of technology. The driven shoot involved a group of men – the 'guns' – being positioned in a line at certain distances apart, perhaps behind some sort of cover. Servants or locals, called beaters, would then begin walking toward them across country or through woods making a noise and a disturbance, to drive birds into the air in the direction of the guns. Because these birds were not wild but had been bred in numbers by gamekeepers within the local woods, there would be a great many of them (King George V killed more than a thousand in a single day – though this was roughly a quarter of the total 'bag' – on his estate at Sandringham). Those doing the shooting needed concentration and accuracy to bring them down. They also needed more than one shotgun to do so. They would therefore have a pair of these guns. While they used one, a servant acting as loader would prepare the other and have it ready for them to exchange. This was a job often undertaken by a gentleman's valet.

Some wildlife was difficult to breed in semi-captivity. The grouse live don the open moors of Yorkshire or the Scottish Highlands. It was shot in the same manner by men largely hidden from sight behind waist-high ramparts of turf or heather. The season for this sport began, and begins, on the twelfth of August ('the glorious twelfth' – restaurants still vie to have grouse on the table as quickly as possible after the season starts). The sport was so popular among aristocrats, millionaires and parliamentarians that the social season ended with the start of grouse-shooting and the upper class, more or less en masse, travelled northward to enjoy the autumn on the open moors. Amid the mountainous Scottish landscape they could pursue another hunting ritual – the stalking and shooting of stags. This was the most difficult of field sports. It involved getting as close as possible to one of these noble beasts without being seen or smelled, and waiting with utmost patience for the moment at which to fire a single shot (there would usually be no opportunity for a second). The work was largely done by a local gamekeeper, who would advise and, if necessary bully, the stalker into position and ensure he kept still and quiet. To crawl on one's belly across a rough landscape and then lie, perhaps for hours, among the rocks and rain and midges, knowing that unless one had the ability of a sniper this effort might be wasted, would not strike everyone as pleasurable. Nevertheless it was another chance for British gentlemen to throw off their sedentary lifestyle and engage in battle against nature.

The Industrial Revolution had produced, by the middle of the nineteenth century, a larger number of rich people than there had ever before been in Britain. As was natural in a nation that had always followed its aristocracy, these new arrivals wanted all the trappings of gentility – schooling in the right places, marriage into the class above, and the traditional symbols of status that represented security and commanded respect. Of these, a country house was seen as the most essential. Its surrounding acres, implying long-established status, could represent even greater prestige than the house itself. There was thus a huge increase in the number of country seats, and in the ranks of the rural landowners who occupied them, appeared at local events, and sought the traditional posts as Lord-Lieutenant and Member of Parliament. It is ironic that the middle classes in transition should have aped so assiduously the lifestyle and the trappings of a social class whose political influence was, at that very moment, losing ground to the bourgeoisie, but as the industrial and commercial magnates assumed greater power and influence, they largely succeeded in integrating, though it commonly took three generations to do so. It was thought necessary for the children of the man who founded the fortune to have grown up with the right education, and therefore with the right friends, marriage connections and leisure pursuits, before *their* children could be on equal terms with older families.

It should not be forgotten that religion too played an important role in the reshaping of the nineteenth-century aristocracy and gentry, which had until the end of the Regency been known for their wildness and self-indulgence. Two things had changed the moral climate; one was a gradually spreading religious revival that had originated with the 'Clapham Sect' surrounding the MP William Wilberforce and his friends, and which had focused originally on agitation to abolish slavery. The early decades of the century became a time of conspicuous piety and domestic virtue, and this state of affairs, given periodic boosts by further Christian re-vivals and the cult of respectability, continued for decades, well into the second half of Victoria's reign.

The second element originated with the Queen herself. In 1837 the last of the unpopular Hanoverian monarchs, William IV (King since 1830), was succeeded by an eighteen-year-old girl. Demure and dutiful, she was naturally a stark contrast to the older men who had been her predecessors, and the Court over which she presided became a radically different place. With her marriage to Albert of Saxe-Coburg-Gotha in 1840, the Royal Family became 'role models' for domestic virtue, characterized by unimpeachable morals, earnest adherence to duty and the dutiful pursuit of knowledge. Albert's inspired leadership in establishing the Great Exhibition, and the national museums that were built with the profits from it, demonstrated the serious tenor of their lives.

As is well known, Victoria and Albert were devoted to each other and to their children (they were to have nine), in a manner that was highly unusual among ruling families or even aristocrats at a time when marriages were often arranged. Because Society took its cue from the Royal Court, domestic virtue and family life became fashionable, and largely remained so for the rest of the century. Not only the Queen's outlook and behaviour but that of the bourgeoisie – whom she and her husband resembled in their attitudes and values – became the accepted norm. The great families became duller and worthier, and to some extent their homes reflected this, though such conformity was often only skin-deep.

The architectural fashion for baronial castles, with all their connotations of pride and power, gave way to the 'Tudorbethan' manor (a combination of Tudor and Elizabethan, though Elizabeth had of course been a Tudor). The originals of such houses, as we have seen, represented a step forward in a land that was by then safe enough not to need drawbridges or battlements, and the replicas, copying the architectural language of that time, sought to represent the characteristics perceived as belonging to that time: prosperity, hospitality, comfort and national ascendancy. The reigns of Elizabeth (1558–1603) and her cousin and heir James I (1603–25) represented another 'golden age' in the history of the English country house. Genuine examples of such buildings were a hallowed feature of the landscape. The revival of these forms was a conscious attempt not only to imply long lineage but to link the present with a previous era of greatness.

Highclere Castle in Hampshire, known throughout

the world as the setting for the television series *Downton Abbey*, is not untypical in its history. It is the ancestral home of the Earls of Carnarvon. They have occupied the site since 1679, having bought it from the Bishops of Winchester, who had owned it for many centuries before that. They originally lived in a brick house but in the late eighteenth century decided to create a more modern structure – country houses, as much as clothes, could fall out of fashion, and families did not want to be seen to have outdated tastes. The Regency house that was built on the site was to last less than a lifetime before it too was demolished, to be replaced with the present one.

The new Highclere was started in 1838, the year that the nineteen-year-old Princess Victoria was crowned and thus the beginning of the great Victorian age. It took until 1878 to complete fully. The original architect was Sir Charles Barry, better known for his work on the Houses of Parliament, which were constructed at exactly the same time. Barry worked in the Italianate manner then much in vogue (his Foreign Office buildings in London's Whitehall are perhaps the country's best-known example of this) and a square campanile or lookout tower was the most distinctive feature of such designs. Highclere has, of course, such a central tower, though the style of the building is what might be called Houses of Parliament Gothic rather than Mediterranean villa.

It is worth remembering, however, that once a family like the Carnarvons had attained the status of landed or titled aristocracy, there was no guarantee that they would stay there. Indolence or profligacy could easily ruin a fortune, especially among those who gambled heavily. Others could be unlucky with their investments as in the previous century's 'South Sea Bubble'. The rise of some families was therefore counterbalanced by the fall of others. Down the centuries there were always country houses or landed estates coming on the market, together with their contents – it was perfectly possible to buy at auction more than enough ancestors to decorate your walls.

One of the most sentimental of Victorian genre paintings captures this notion. R. B. Martineau's *The Last Day in the Old Home* was painted in 1862 and is now on display at Tate Britain. It was painted at Godinton House (also known as Godinton Park) in Kent, an archetypal English manor that for centuries had been the home of the Toke family. The carved Jacobean fireplace and the bay window Martineau depicted are still instantly recognizable to present-day visitors. In the picture, the paintings and suits of armour are in the process of being packed as the young owner and his son drink a final toast to the house, putting a brave face on the loss of their heritage. His wife looks less sanguine and his mother, in conversation perhaps with the family solicitor, is distraught. This fate will have befallen many families during the Victorian era, for we must remember that agriculture was in almost perpetual decline throughout the reign, and that those who depended upon it for their sole income could be faced with ruin. Had coal been found beneath the ground, as it was by the Earls of Home beneath their Scottish Borders home The Hirsel, perhaps the family could have stayed, retaining their birthright even if their view was spoiled by slag heaps. The young boy who will now not inherit the estate may be more fortunate than he realizes, for he would have been forced to take on further years of struggle and perhaps misery as he tried to keep the estate going, dreading – as his father perhaps did – that he would be the one to let go of it all.

It is always worth remembering that the apparently timeless life of a great country house was not – whatever its inhabitants or the public may have believed – by any means a perpetual state of affairs. Financial ruin could end this agreeable existence remarkably quickly. The loss of heirs through war or illness or accident – for many of these wealthy young men enjoyed risky hobbies such as hunting, motor racing or flying – could bring an end to a family's tenure when no one was left to carry on. Richard Harpur-Crewe, for instance, who would have inherited Calke Abbey, died of cancer in 1921; Antony, Viscount Knebworth and heir to the 2nd Earl of Lytton, was killed while flying in 1933 with the Royal Auxiliary Air Force. It is important therefore to remember that there was never, for the families concerned, any room for complacency about occupying a country house. Many families may have enjoyed a solid income from their estates, but they were at the mercy of inflation, falling land values and increased taxation. Every generation had to struggle to keep the establishment going, and not the least of their concerns was providing for the servants who lived on their land and worked for them.

Wealth had by now decisively passed from the old aristocracy to the commercial and industrial elite. Their brains and their products had made this 'nation of shopkeepers' (Napoleon's phrase) the wealthiest country in the world. One strength of the British tradition, source of its renewed vigour and continuity, was that the aristocracy was never a closed circle. In many continental countries a man was either born to a title or could never hope for one. In Britain a successful, ambitious man could earn his way in. The upper echelons of society were constantly being replenished. There would often be sniping and sneering by the snobbish (when, for example, in the late nineteenth century there were several ennoblements of wealthy brewers, they became known as 'the beerage'), but the openness of the 'best circles' in Britain was given fresh impetus by the readiness of Albert, Prince of Wales (later Edward VII) to consort with the newly rich.

It became common, in an age when politics was more cliqueish than it is today, to have political house parties – gatherings at aristocratic seats whose owners were Whig or Tory partisans, at which the great men of the age would spend the time between Saturday and Monday discussing the issues of the moment and making decisions that would affect the nation and the Empire. One distinguished stately home – Warwick Castle, the home of the Greville family – hosted such a weekend party in the summer of 1898. A century later the Castle was owned by the Tussauds Group, proprietors of the famous waxworks, and they re-created the 1898 weekend in a series of tableaux, set in the precise rooms in which the guests had slept, dined, played cards and talked politics. The guest of honour was the Prince of Wales, and his son, the Duke of York, was also present. So were Lord Curzon, Field Marshal Lord Roberts, Winston Churchill and the singer Clara Butt, who performed to entertain the guests. Sadly this imaginative and vivid exhibition is no longer there, but it gave, as no other display could have, the perfect picture of a vanished age of opulence and influence.

The Victorian country seats that sprang up to host such august gatherings all over the United Kingdom will, in many cases, have invited ridicule for their architectural pretensions. The use of Gothic architecture to suggest that the building – and the family – had been there for generations, if not centuries, already was widely mocked at the time, but gradually these overbearing arrivals settled into the landscape. Their stone or brick, weathered to a mellow patina and perhaps overgrown with ivy, has made their appearance much less abrasive than formerly, and many of them have earned the affection of visitors and architectural writers alike, either for their pleasing general aspect or because they are important examples of the style of their time. However, passing years cannot help some buildings, which simply defy admiration. A recent visitor to one house, the writer John Pearson, commented on his first glimpse of Joyce Grove, the Victorian family seat of the Fleming banking family, in a manner that suggests how such houses are viewed from our own perspective:

> There are ugly houses and ugly houses, but this is a monster, an architectural tyrannosaurus which has blundered into these Oxfordshire beech woods from another age and somehow become preserved, dead but completely intact. As you peer at this house with its fierce red walls, its elaborate portico, its jagged roofs and chimneys and cornices, you murmur to yourself – who?

Rather more successful is Tyntesfield, the vast neo-Gothic house at Wraxall in Somerset built for William

Gibbs (1790–1875), a member of an old West Country merchant family who made a fortune by importing guano to England from South America. He wanted precisely the sort of grand country seat that was enjoyed by the traditional aristocracy, and it was built for him by the architect John Norton. The house was occupied by four generations of the family before its upkeep – it has 43 bedrooms – proved too great an expense for them. As at Calke Abbey, the National Trust took it over, after a fundraising campaign in which the public was urged to donate by the argument that this was a very rare survival of house, estate, contents, gardens and estate buildings, all intact – and additionally by the rumour that the house might otherwise be bought by the singer Kylie Minogue. Again as at Calke, the public greatly enjoyed the fact that Tyntesfield was filled with a random collection of domestic objects, seemingly left as they had been when the last family member departed. There were children's toys – for a Victorian nursery is a feature much loved by country-house visitors – and kitchens and servants' quarters filled with mysterious implements or quaintly old-fashioned cleaning products. The family rooms boast enough artistic treasures to satisfy the aesthete, but the house's chief interest lies in the fact that it reflects the aspirations and outlook of the mercantile class that built Britain's nineteenth-century prosperity through overseas trade.

Age alone does not make a house interesting. There are medieval, Tudor and Elizabethan houses that, for all their authenticity, attract less public enthusiasm than later examples that have fascinating collections, or beautiful gardens, or associations with notable personalities. Sometimes, though rarely, it is the collection within rather than the building or the gardens that is the house's chief 'selling point'. Littlecote House in Berkshire – a magnificent Tudor mansion bought in the 1980s by a prominent businessman – was and is renowned for its collection of armour dating from the English Civil Wars. The owner decided to sell this, and there was an immediate nationwide campaign, led by the Royal Armouries, to raise funds and save it for the nation. All over Britain in the middle of that decade there were posters urgently pleading for donations before time ran out. In the end Littlecote's owner, perhaps pleased or surprised by the amount of interest aroused, decided to keep the armour and display it, and it remains there today though the house is now a hotel. Objects can sometimes take on a life of their own.

As in the previous century there were architects – or firms of architects – who specialized in country-house building. They could provide from an extensive catalogue of historic styles any period look, or combination of them, that a client wished. They could also advise on the type of house that would best fit a particular landscape, be it the Thames Valley, the Midlands or the Scottish Highlands. Some architects, notably William Burges (1827–81), worked in an almost pure medieval style. The houses he built for the 3rd Marquess of Bute (1847–1900) were a dream worthy of Ludwig of Bavaria. Cardiff Castle (commissioned because Bute was a major local landowner and builder of the nearby docks) was not intended as a residence but as a civic headquarters. Nevertheless Burges, taking the sparse remains of an ancient castle as the basis for his building, created what looked like a fanciful, whimsical medieval dwelling. It was what an ideal house in the Middle Ages might have been like had the builders then had the technology available in the nineteenth century, and it included such modern refinements as a 'winter smoking room'.

Castell Coch was a smaller, private residence built in the hills above Cardiff, used as a home by Bute and his wife (they had other country residences elsewhere, so that this was for them an occasional retreat). Again it used an existing ruin as the basis for a rebuild that was more elaborate and imaginative than the medieval masons could have dreamed of. Burges, in common with others who worked in the historicist idiom, did not just erect the shell but created all the interior fittings as well. Burges designed furniture, wallcoverings and washbasins for the castle – the antithesis, of course, the way the English country house traditionally developed, with elements added by each new generation. Though a hundred years earlier, the Adam brothers had designed interiors as well as exteriors, they had never shown such attention to detail. The hallmark of the art-architects of the late nineteenth and early twentieth centuries was to set their stamp on every room and feature of the house they were creating – to make of it a work of art, complete in every aspect.

Another change the Victorians introduced to house design was the new emphasis placed on the nursery. Despite the oft-quoted stricture that 'children should be seen and not heard', which is wrongly assumed to sum up the attitude of nineteenth-century parents, this was an age that set very considerable store by family life and the image of domesticity. Children were no longer regarded, as they had been in previous generations, as miniature adults. There had for a long time been schoolrooms in country houses, but the nursery is a Victorian creation – though perhaps spartan, even grim in its furnishings, its fireplace and its scattered toys and books can render it so cosy, comfortable and evocative that many houses have still preserved them, as intact as possible. They are frequently the room that visitors most enjoy seeing. The nursery with its scattered toys and books (for the amount of reading matter published entirely for juveniles was another striking characteristic of the time) soon became an institution.

The great hall, a distinguishing feature of medieval houses where it was used for dining, underwent a revival as Victorian architects reintroduced it to country houses. Because of the nineteenth century's rediscovery of morality, many houses segregated male and female guests into separate corridors of bedrooms that might well be divided from each other by the whole width of the house's central block. The great hall offered a magnificent setting for mixed social gatherings, where tea would be served and indoor games played, or for assemblies before dinner.

Another popular element in Victorian house design was the conservatory, a sort of hothouse in which exotic flora could be placed, providing a winter garden. The Victorians loved these spaces not only for the facilities they provided – the opportunity for light and modest exercise in inclement weather, and the opportunities to display collections of plants, ferns, palm trees (very fashionable at one time, as can be seen for instance in the paintings of James Tissot from the 1870s and 80s) – but also for their novelty value. It was only through recent advances in construction using glass and iron that such buildings had become possible. The Crystal Palace, built by Joseph Paxton for the Great Exhibition that was held in London's Hyde Park in 1851, was the wonder of the mid-Victorian age. Its prototype can still be seen at a country house – Chatsworth – for Paxton was employed there and owed his subsequent advancement to the greenhouse that he constructed for the Duke of Devonshire. The Great Exhibition made iron and glass fashionable building materials, and every home could, as it were, now have its own fragment of the Crystal Palace. The conservatory was often reached by French windows leading from a drawing room or dining room.

The manner in which people dined underwent a major change in the century's latter decades. The traditional method of serving at a dinner table was for every dish to be placed in front of the master of the house, who would carve the meats and divide everything into portions, with servants passing the plates. The new fashion, which had become standard among elegant householders by the 1880s, was to dine *à la Russe*. This was a means of serving by which every dish would be carried round by footmen so that the guests could be served at their places rather than having plates brought to them. Though the adoption of this was gradual, it saved so much general confusion that it soon became the only way to serve at formal dinners, and has remained so ever since. The old way of doing things had meant that a servant had to be present for each diner, standing behind their chair. Though this was no longer necessary, the sight of liveried footmen thus arrayed in rows was impressive, and heightened the sense of occasion (as it still does at state banquets in royal palaces). Many hosts therefore wished to keep footmen in numbers suitable for this display, even though – as was commonplace – additional men had to be hired from agencies to supplement the family's own servants, and all of them were often underemployed.

The drawing room became the setting, by late Victorian times, for the 'morning call', curiously always made in the afternoon. These were never such a feature of country houses as of town dwellings, for the obvious reason that where houses were set farther apart and distances were greater it was not possible to call upon so many ladies in the space of an afternoon. It was especially pointless in that a polite call should be of no more than fifteen minutes' duration and should not involve the recipient of it in the offer of any refreshment. (This was because a caller could not be constantly eating and drinking – they might have ten calls to make!)

The custom of taking port and cigars after dinner was not native to England. It came from Germany and was first introduced in honour of the Duke of Sussex, one of the sons of King George III, because he had lived a number of years in Germany. His example was to be endorsed by Queen Victoria's husband, Prince Albert, a few decades later. In a pre-celebrity age it was the aristocracy, and even more the monarchy, which initiated social trends.

The notion of a house being divided into male and female territory was not entirely new, but it became more pronounced in the Victorian age and in the decades that followed. The things that set the sexes apart were their conversation and their leisure interests. Men wanted to smoke, and could not do so in mixed company because the habit would be objectionable to ladies, who until the very end of the country-house era did not smoke in public or, for the most part, in private. Men played billiards, which women on the whole did not. Men went shooting and hunting and, though women did these things too, their strength and aptitude and therefore expertise were not considered great enough to be taken seriously. Men wanted to talk politics and money, which were not considered subjects on which women could have informed opinions. While the men were engaged in these activities, their wives and sisters and daughters sat in other parts of the house, immersed in idle gossip or in looking at the pictures, browsing in the library or writing letters. They must frequently have been bored to distraction by the company, especially if they met the same friends and relatives week after week while visiting different houses, but for members of their class this would have been a common experience.

One thing that such girls had often done was to travel abroad to spend a few months, or years, at a finishing school on the Continent. This was considered an essential means of giving them some exposure to the polite world. For decades there had been English girls' schools in European cities whose expatriate population could support them, and pupils might either stay in a residential environment or with a family considered to be suitable hosts. This practice was surprisingly similar to arrangements made for young people today, except that there was more emphasis on formality. One region that hosted thousands of young women in the years before the First World War was the German Kingdom of Saxony. Its capital, Dresden, had a long-established British colony. It was a city famous for its art collections, and was in fact a favoured honeymoon destination for Anglo-Saxons. In the television drama *Upstairs, Downstairs* the daughter of the Bellamy family, Elizabeth, is sent to Frau Beck's in Dresden to spend a few months acquiring social polish (instead she returns filled with radical social ideas and half-understood philosophy that puts off the young men she meets). Young women of a more intellectual bent might stay in Erfurt, the seat of a famous university. If they were musical they would opt for Leipzig. Once the home of Bach, it was a city entirely given over to music. Here there was a social scene based on concerts and recitals. The cafés were filled with musicians and music students, every other man seemed to be a teacher of piano or violin. This was a Germany that seemed far removed from the sabre-rattling of the Prussians, a country of picnics and excursions and health cures, in which even the smallest city seemed to boast an opera house. It was a place in which many young women spent a golden interlude before returning to 'come out' in the London Season.

By the end of the century the country house – as can be seen from the examples built by Lutyens or Sir Reginald Blomfield – was a less rigidly organized, punctilious and formal, and a more relaxed, place. There had been a rationalizing of design and function so that the new country houses being built were designed primarily for the comfort of those who often did their work elsewhere and came to them only for relaxation. The architecture of a house like

Chatsworth, for instance, would have been equally appropriate in the midst of a city, and its elegant, embellished façade may look splendid but stands in contrast to, rather than fitting in with, the adjacent landscape. Later houses were more consciously harmonious with their surroundings. As well as looking as though they had been there for centuries, their vernacular styles were intended to reflect the virtues of the countryside, the simplicity of life there, the sense of deep cultural roots, the closeness to nature and the rhythm of the seasons. There was about them a staged unpretentiousness that sometimes became pretentious. They were also designed to catch the sun, their surfaces were simplified by plain oak fixtures and areas of white paint. As is often the case, this move towards simplicity occurred at the same time as a downturn in the fortunes of many landowning families.

The arrival of cheap imported corn from North America led to a lasting depression in British agriculture, and suddenly the prestige associated with land ownership – or at least the power that had always accompanied it – was gone. Many families, who had invested generations of time and effort in their estates, found themselves having to sell. A number of estates went to the new plutocratic class that had gradually wrested control of real power and wealth from the oldest aristocratic families. Other houses, inconveniently large or not aesthetically pleasing, failed to find a buyer. What some observers find surprising is that, throughout history, so many country houses have been demolished. This is not a fate that usually befalls more modest rural homes when they lose their original owners or purpose. An old yeoman's house, a stable block, a former windmill . . . new functions can be found for all of these, and they can be converted without great difficulty. A country house is different. It is usually too big for a single family, who do not need the space and cannot afford the upkeep. It is difficult to get to, surrounded as it should be by acres of park or farmland. The bills for heating it, without which the damp could be catastrophic, can be immense, and so can the maintenance of huge expanses of roof, which cannot be allowed to leak. Many families who inhabit such structures retreat to one part of them – a single wing, or even a few rooms – because that is all they can afford to inhabit. The bigger the house, the more acute these difficulties are, and the more thoroughly uneconomical it is to maintain. So the image of a placid, timeless way of life going on amid archetypal English surroundings is, in the majority of cases, a sham. This was just as true in the Victorian and Edwardian eras as it is today. Beneath the tranquil surface there were usually grievous economic problems to be solved by each new generation.

One very obvious solution, during the black years of the nineteenth-century agricultural depression, was to marry money. This could mean the daughter of a millionaire soap-manufacturer, though there would be a danger of the aristocratic family which accepted her losing caste. The United States, whose economy had been one of the strongest in the world even by the time of the American Revolution, had now surpassed any other country in the world in wealth, displacing the United Kingdom which had previously occupied that position thanks to the Industrial Revolution. America was, after its Civil War (1861–5), enjoying a so-called 'Gilded Age', in which individual fortunes were made on a scale that dwarfed anything seen before. Steel and railroads, shipping lines, and even exported grain that was causing distress to British agriculture meant that the US dollar could buy the world. To make an alliance with a successful American family, whose members were often socially ambitious, seemed a simple solution to impecunious English aristocrats.

In Edith Wharton's novel *The Buccaneers* (1938) she somewhat ruthlessly depicts the young women of eastern America whose mothers want them – and indeed who themselves want – to make good marriages and to rise in Society. This proves extremely difficult – even humiliating – in a country then in the process of forming its own aristocracy. The newer the institution, the more snobbish and restrictive it seems to be. Failing to make headway at home, the girls come to England, where they are resented as upstarts by some, and hated by the British girls with whom they are competing for husbands. Nevertheless they find fewer barriers to advancement in an older society that is willing to accept wealthy incomers, and they succeed in marrying, not least because the men find their company more amusing than that of conventionally brought up young English-women. One girl becomes a duchess, though she quickly finds that her marriage is a matter of surface affection only and her husband is in fact homosexual.

In reality, American girls of precisely this sort crossed the Atlantic and successfully joined the British aristoc-racy. In most cases a marriage was arranged in which their primary role was to shore up, with the parental dollars, the crumbling home of a titled family. But not invariably . . . Mary Leiter, the daughter of a millionaire from Washington DC, became engaged to Lord Curzon in 1891. Theirs was a love match, and the couple remained happy together until her death in 1905 (from the effects of the drains at their official residence). Her money was to fund Curzon's political career – he became Viceroy of India and Foreign Secretary, and very nearly Prime Minister.

Another instance, far better chronicled, was the straightforward money-for-title alliance of Consuelo Vanderbilt with 'Sunny', 9th Duke of Marlborough, which took place in New York in July 1894. The choice of husband, after several possibilities had been considered, was made by Consuelo's mother, Alva. She dragooned the reluctant girl into marrying (Consuelo was in love with another man, who had been forced from the scene). Marlborough himself was indifferent. He too had already cast his affections elsewhere and was interested only in furthering his family and saving the enormous Blenheim Palace from decay. The marriage was a pretence and it ended in divorce within a decade. Consuelo moved abroad and created another life for herself.

It is worth remembering that it was not only taxes and the cost of maintenance that could threaten the continuity of a country house and its way of life. There was the same danger that had always existed: that the extravagance of an owner, or of his eldest son, would cause the family to have to sell. As always, the first things to go would be possessions – the contents – and the actual structure would be sold only as a last resort. In the library at Blenheim Palace is an immense organ, installed in Victoria's reign. One reason for putting it there was to make the room look less bare, for more than 200 paintings had had to be sold by the eighth duke to pay off debts.

Such arrangements often worked for a generation or two, preserving the house and its treasures for half a century or so, but they could not usually provide a permanent solution, and later members of the family would have to resume the same process. In the drama *Downton Abbey*, the Earl of Grantham belongs precisely to the generation of young English landowners who married into America's dollar aristocracy in order to maintain an ancestral home and pass it on to future generations. His wife has always been well aware of her role in this process, yet they have a fortunate marriage (in everything except the birth of a male heir) and a good deal of mutual affection. This was a not untypical situation. The culture shock for the new brides was often shocking, though the etiquette they encountered in Britain was as nothing to what they would have found in some other old European societies, such as Spain or Austria–Hungary. The British aristocracy proved flexible enough to absorb these newcomers, and the women in turn revitalized to some extent the world that they joined, so that the mix was on the whole a healthy and a positive one. Some went on to make great contributions to national life. Lady Randolph Churchill, another American trophy-bride, paid for and ran a hospital ship during the Second Boer or South African War, as did her compatriot and relative, the Duchess of Marlborough. These ladies were also credited with defusing political tension when in 1895 Britain and the United States almost went to war over a territorial dispute in Venezuela.

There was in fact nothing unheard of in the notion of new fortunes coming to the rescue of old ones, of the newly rich putting up monuments to their own success, or indeed of the public ridiculing them for doing so. Piccadilly, the quaintly named street in London's West End, derives its name from one such case in the seventeenth century. Robert Baker was a manufacturer of piccadills, the type of starched, stand-up linen collars that were in fashion for both men and women in the time of Shakespeare. Having made a fortune from them, Baker bought land to the west of London in what was then open countryside and built a large house. Since the English love a lord but are guilty of a good deal of vicarious snobbery, they laughed at his pretensions and christened his home 'Piccadilly Hall'. The nearby thoroughfare acquired the same name by association, and an official attempt, later in the seventeenth century, to rename it Portugal Street came too late. The original name had already stuck.

With the advent of international money to Britain and a new breed of successful tycoons, rich enough to live in a grand country house only at weekends, the role of the old landed aristocracy might have been threatened – but for one thing. The landowning class may have been losing money, just as earlier in the century it had lost political power, yet because the lifestyle it enjoyed was seen as the best that a wealthy, influential and historic country could offer, the established forms of aristocratic country life were eagerly seized upon and emulated by others, who did their best to keep up customs and standards of behaviour. From the outside, the privileged world of the English country house could seem quite unchanged.

In January 1897 the magazine *Country Life* was published for the first time. It captured, through sympathetic articles and evocative pictures, the world of traditional rural certainties that had in fact all but vanished, while simultaneously becoming the focus of widespread longing. This periodical, which continues to flourish today, was read by rural gentry and nostalgic 'townies' in equal measure. The British countryside had largely lost its role as provider of food for the nation, through the importing of cheap American corn, and beef and mutton frozen and shipped to its shores from as far away as Argentina and New Zealand. The rural landscape became, for the wealthy and the visiting townsman, a place of leisure and of sentimental quaintness. Commercial and industrial magnates, whose factories were shrouding the cities in grime and smoke, sought escape in their own rural idyll – complete with all the mod cons their new money could buy. It has been estimated that between 1835 and 1889 500 or so country houses were either built or restored. More than half of these were for the new class of wealthy families. To build one required the very considerable sum of £10,000. The cost of hiring servants for such a house was almost as much – about £8,000 per year to pay the wages of the 170 or so staff that would be necessary to run a medium-sized country seat.

The houses built for successful businessmen were frequently ugly, or at best unimaginative. This was because many of the owners had little aesthetic sense, and saw their homes only in terms of practicalities. These were men whose fortunes had been based on knowing what they wanted, and getting it. Instead of asking an architect for ideas, they laid down a series of demands that the building's designer was obliged to incorporate, or else lose the commission. Few eminent or fashionable architects would have been willing to be bullied in that manner, and thus the ones who agreed to the work were either unremarkable or were unable to have much influence over the result. They gave their clients what they required, but the houses they built have not been cherished by posterity. Typical of them is the somewhat startling Overstone Hall in Northamptonshire, built by W. M. Teulon for Samuel Lloyd, a wealthy banker.

Where many derided these newer mansions as pure pastiche of past ages a number of them, because of the style in which they were built, have subsequently come to be regarded as treasures in their own right, examples of a time that saw significant achievements in building and decorating, and worthy of comparison with the great houses of other ages. Some of the finest properties in the keeping of English Heritage, Friends of Scottish Monuments or the National Trust in fact date from these years of late Victorian and Edwardian taste.

Widespread industrialization and the mass production of even artistic items by machinery, which had been celebrated at the time of the Great Exhibition in 1851 as a wonder of technology and a source of national pride, had by the end of the century led to a reaction. This was expressed in the philosophy of the art critic John Ruskin (1819–1900), and by one of his disciples, the socialist

William Morris (1834–96), who had initially thought of becoming an architect himself but who instead developed into a polymathic creator who simply taught himself to work in any of the media he wished to practise. He became an extremely proficient artist and craftsman, and founded a loose endeavour devoted to precisely these things – the Arts and Crafts Movement. This sought to benefit both the creator and the consumer of artistic work. By restoring the practice of hand-made craftwork – by having furniture and fittings laboriously carved by experts rather than produced by machine, for instance – Morris sought to return to craftsmen the satisfaction and status of which mass production had robbed them, as well as giving the public artefacts that they could appreciate for their excellence. In keeping with Morris's socialist views, he hoped that such works could be put within reach of the wider public, who would be educated by contact with them.

Unfortunately this notion was simply not practical. The work that he, his associates and those influenced by them carried out was so labour-intensive, and the materials they used so costly, that the objects remained exclusive and expensive. The only people who could easily afford such work – at least in quantities sufficient to decorate a house – were the wealthy, and many of the examples of Arts and Crafts architecture or decoration that are admired in situ today are in country houses. While Morris did not therefore succeed in his initial objective, he and his followers created along the way a style that instantly appealed to artists, architects and craftsmen throughout the world, as well as to the general public. Arts and Crafts style has been widely admired and copied ever since, and – both in the lofty notions that inspired it and the objects it produced – is one of the great achievements of the Victorian era. Examples of buildings inspired by it can be found as far away as India and China. It was also extremely influential in Europe, where it had an impact on the design of houses in Scandinavia, Germany and Italy in particular. In an echo of the eighteenth century, when the informality of the English landscape park had been widely copied on the Continent, so the Arts and Crafts interior, with its spacious and uncluttered feel and its simple, basic use of materials and colours, was widely emulated.

The United States quickly developed its own Arts and Crafts Movement, producing specialist architects who built notable country houses, as well as the type of artistic commune (the Roycroft Workshops in New York State) that applied the philosophy to narrower fields such as furniture making, tapestry and bookbinding.

It is a commonplace to describe Victorian country houses as 'ugly', yet the Arts and Crafts examples of domestic architecture, equally Victorian, are not generally regarded in this way. The earlier styles of the Queen's reign, pastiches of Georgian or Gothic or Italianate design (her own summer home, Osborne on the Isle of Wight, was a notable and influential example of the latter), have all suffered from reversals in the popular perception of what is considered tasteful and desirable. The principles of design advocated and practised by the Arts and Crafts Movement meant that, by the time of Victoria's death, both owners and builders of new houses were a great deal more sensitive to qualities such as harmony, comfort and practicality. Lutyens, their doyen, made a point of using materials such as old bricks and weathered, unstained oak that would blend a house into the landscape around it. The imposing country seat, bristling with towers and battlements, stamping its authority – whether real or aspirational – over the surrounding fields, was now a thing of the past. The style of its successors was one of comfortable domesticity, expressed in chimney stacks, leaded windows, half-timbering and bay windows. The entrances were not designed to intimidate, and the interiors, which commonly lacked a great hall (there was no need for such a thing, since there were no tenants to entertain to dinner), was not laid out geometrically with long corridors but in the traditional manner around open courtyards, and filled with quaint corners and oddities.

There are wonderful surviving examples of such houses, such as Blackwell in the Lake District. It was built between 1898 and 1900 by the Arts and Crafts architect M. H. Baillie Scott for the Manchester brewer Sir Edward Holt. Scott made use of local resources (the roofs are of Westmorland slate) and local craftsmen, who understood both the materials they were using and the building techniques of the region. The chimney stacks, for instance, are rounded, as was customary on farmhouses in the locality. The first thing that strikes a visitor is the utter simplicity of the house's exterior. There is no ornament, and the windows do not even have sills or hoods. The walls are roughcast and painted white, making the house conspicuous over long distances. Blackwell's design is as basic inside as out. The colours are light and the lines are simple. The woodwork – panelling, stair-rails, shelving, floors – is of golden, polished oak. The rooms are dominated by large and comfortable inglenook fireplaces. Rooms, especially the drawing room, are angled to make maximum use of sunlight, and some very stylized stained glass allows this to spread beautiful splashes of colour across walls and floors. Despite its deliberate Tudor references, Blackwell is a far cry from the country house of many Englishmen's daydreams, yet it must surely win more genuine affection than the overwhelming and draughty halls of some of England's Baroque mansions.

Rodmarton Manor in Gloucestershire is another house that is a landmark of this style, though it was built a generation later. It was constructed between 1909 and 1929 by the architect and designer Ernest Barnsley in collaboration with the couple who commissioned it, Claud and Margaret Biddulph. This was not an aristocratic seat, and nor was it the home of an industrial magnate. It was instead a development of something that has already been hinted at in this chapter – a country house conceived as an expression of idealism. The builders of this house were aiming to create beauty in a style appropriate to the surroundings, and to live in a comfortable, unpretentious place that made reference to the virtues of rural life in some ideal 'Tudorbethan' past. Indeed while Blackwell could not be mistaken for anything other than a modern house of the 1890s, Rodmarton looks like a genuine Elizabethan manor even when seen from close quarters. The major objective of the builders, however, was to celebrate a sense of artistry and community.

The Biddulphs became friends of Ernest Barnsley, an idealistic designer and architect who had founded, at

Sapperton near Cirencester, a commune of artisans (mostly from the East End of London) to work in traditional styles. The project was begun in 1893 and would continue well into the following century. The men and women working there produced wooden furniture and fittings, metalwork and ceramics of real ingenuity and originality, and Rodmarton became a showplace for their skills. The notion that it represented a community is emphasized by the circular lawn at the front of the building. This looks like a village green, and was intended to function as one. It served as an outdoor gathering place for all who lived or worked at the house. Another of its features, unusual by the time it was built but a further affirmation of community, is the chapel. Though ecclesiastical decoration is an opportunity for craftsmen to exercise imagination and creativity, the room is as simple in design as the rest of the building. Like other Arts and Crafts houses, Rodmarton is all of a piece and all of one period. Its importance lies not only in its status as a supreme example of a style that was particularly strong and influential in the history of English building, but also in the fact that it was designed for the entire community that would live in it and not simply its owners.

There were exceptions to this ground-breaking new approach, houses deliberately built to express a symmetry and order and grandeur in keeping with the Edwardian imperial heyday. The most striking example is Manderston, built for the merchant Sir James Miller in the Scottish lowlands south of Edinburgh. This house, once again cherished because it represents a single epoch and a single owner's vision, was completed in 1905. It is so much 'of its time' – considered the finest 'stately home' in Britain of the opening years of the twentieth century, despite being the antithesis of the Lutyens-inspired trend for homely country residences – that it was used in 2002 as the setting for the reality television series *The Edwardian Country House*. Its inspiration is drawn from the eighteenth century, its neo-Georgian exterior crowned with urns and balustrade, and its entrance hall dominated by a staircase that was copied from the Petit Trianon at Versailles.

There were other houses that bucked the trend by aiming at grandeur. Cragside was a modelling, by the great – though in the 1860s still largely unknown – Victorian architect Richard Norman Shaw, of a house already built for William Armstrong, 1st Baron Armstrong. It was scarcely complete before plans were under way to remodel it completely. It is a very homely house, but its majestic setting, as well as its scale and the detail of some of its interiors, makes it grander than many contemporary houses were trying to be.

A great house still required a great number of servants, but by the beginning of the twentieth century, technology was making their lives easier, eliminating some of the dirtiness and drudgery that had consumed so much time and effort.

For instance, with the introduction of radiators and gas fires there was less need for that bane of the housemaid's life, the endless cleaning of grates. Nor was it necessary to waste time and effort on lugging coal upstairs from the cellar. With hot water available from pipes and taps it no longer had to be carried up to bedrooms and bathrooms. The coach

house, formerly a highly important part of the establishment, was now entirely redundant in many households.
The coachman himself had probably had to learn to drive
an automobile, and his assistants – the grooms and stable
boys – had gone entirely or been retrained for other jobs.
Since the chauffeur was also a mechanic, the family's
transportation was now the responsibility of only one
man instead of four or five. The abandoning of oil and
gas lamps meant the loss of another dirty and time-
consuming job and, incidentally, saw the demise of the
'lamp boy', a junior servant who previously had started
a lifetime in service with this lowly task.

The laundry wing was another casualty of changing
times. Larger country houses had always had them, yet
it became very easy to do without. Commercial laundries
could arrange for collection, cleaning and delivery
without the need for servants to do more than sort the
returned clothing and household items, and put them
away. The same became true of many other aspects of
running the household, as grocers and bakers also
delivered, negating to some extent the need for the cook
and housekeeper to work so hard.

Estate Duty was imposed for the first time in 1894,
increasing in 1909 under the Liberal government of
Lloyd George and again in 1919, when the landed classes
had already been badly hit by the wartime loss of family
members. Add to this the increase in income tax, and the
fact that the wages paid to servants were now much
higher than they had been before 1914. Domestic staff,
now highly conscious of the value of their work and of
the opportunities available to them elsewhere, largely
had to be bribed to stay with better conditions than had

previously been available. Householders had, in the decades between the mid-Victorian era and the First World War, almost entirely given up the role they had assumed as moral guardians to their servants. Such attitudes were simply out of fashion, especially after the accession of the notoriously pleasure-loving King Edward VII. His behaviour, and that of his raffish friends, heralded an era of libertinism, with widespread bed-hopping among the guests at country-house parties. It was simply too difficult to pretend that the upper class in general held any moral authority over their employees in the face of such behaviour.

The lifestyle that went with country-house living underwent rapid changes in accordance with new social conditions. Though dinner remained a formal affair and guests still dressed for it, the day's other repasts tended to be more relaxed, especially breakfast, which was normally a sideboard buffet. Dining rooms in newer houses became smaller. Men and women mixed more often and more informally. The morning room, a female bastion, saw much less use than formerly, though its male equivalent, the smoking room, continued to be frequented by men even though both men and women now smoked quite openly around the house. Conservatories, formerly the epitome of Victorian indoor recreation, ceased to be built and would make a comeback only in our own times. They had perhaps come to symbolize for many the stuffiness, both literal and metaphorical, of the era that had passed.

One of the last great country houses to be built in Britain ironically saw a return to the very beginnings of the genre. Castle Drogo was the last castle to be built in

Britain. It was constructed between 1911 and 1931, and was completed and occupied at precisely the time when it became uneconomical to maintain a large country house in England. It is worth examining for other reasons too, for the nature of its owner, his choice of architect and site and building materials all tell us something significant about the world of the country house and the role it plays in the social ambitions of the British.

Julius Drew (1856–1931) was a wealthy grocer. As a young man with an acute business sense, he began a Liverpool grocery at the age of twenty-two and soon established a nationwide chain of shops – the Home and Colonial Stores – that became so profitable he could afford to retire at thirty-three. He had not by any means sprung from nowhere – his family had had modest wealth and social position for several generations – but he wished to achieve the status and the lifestyle of the aristocracy, and he had the financial means to do so. He changed the spelling of his surname to 'Drewe', and employed a genealogist to investigate his family tree. This turned up a connection with a Norman knight called Drogo de Teigne who had held lands in Devon near the River Teign.

Drewe and his family visited the area, and were enchanted. For those who like wild landscapes Dartmoor is not difficult to love, the neat fields and villages on its edges providing a pleasingly domestic counterpoint to the wildness of the neighbouring moor. The family decided to settle there. Drewe purchased several hundred acres that included the rocky outcrop on which the 'ancestral' home was to be built. It would be a castle, and this prominence was precisely the sort of place in which medieval builders would have sited a defensive structure. The 'ancestral home' of the Drewes was to be authentic from the beginning. Not only their home but its surroundings would be made to fit the lineage to which Drewe aspired. The nearby village was persuaded to change its name to Drewsteignton, and the landlord of the local pub obligingly renamed his premises The Drewe Arms. Here was, in somewhat exaggerated form, the newly arrived 'aristocrat's' dream of creating a house that would imply long centuries of occupancy.

The architect chosen was Edwin Lutyens. By 1911, when building began, he was highly sought after and correspondingly busy. He loved romantic buildings and had recently completed a successful, evocative and highly praised restoration of a ruin on Lindisfarne Island, off the coast of Northumberland, creating a comfortable Edwardian country house. Now he was travelling to and fro between England and India, where he was planning and constructing an entire city: the administrative centre of the British Raj, New Delhi. He was, however, delighted to be given the chance to create a castle, and to do so from scratch with the sort of extravagant budget that Drewe could provide.

Unfortunately the funds available were not as limitless as Lutyens had expected. When the site was marked out, Drewe immediately ordered it reduced by half, and the building would, when finished, be only one-third of the size originally envisaged. Costs had to be cut from the beginning, and Lutyens was to be constantly exasperated by major changes that had to be factored in while construction was under way, but nevertheless the result was impressive. Now owned by the National Trust, it is admired by thousands of visitors every year, but its owner was never to see it complete. Julius Drewe died in 1931, the year the building was finished, but at that time not all the rooms were yet habitable.

Because the notion was to build an instant ancestral home, Castle Drogo had to incorporate several architectural styles. The Castle was built with a lack of symmetry that was quite deliberate, to imply that extensions had been tacked on by succeeding owners. The granite exterior seems forbidding and impregnable yet its lack of battlements – only a few turrets are castellated – gives it a curiously modern look. It is, as it was intended to be, an authentic fortress that could actually withstand a siege (in some places its walls are six feet thick). It has usable arrow slits and even a working portcullis. The sense of gradual evolution was evident in the interior details too. The stonework for the fireplace in the entrance hall shows some carvings that appear to be medieval and are clearly unfinished, as if abandoned halfway through by a long-forgotten stonemason.

Inside, the house is a great deal more comfortable than the grim ramparts would lead visitors to expect, yet here also large areas of bare granite are visible. The effect is softened by fittings and furnishings of oak – such as the billiard table and library shelves – designed by Lutyens himself. There is a 'Georgian' sitting room. There are comfortable bedrooms and an elegant library, in styles that suggest the eighteenth, nineteenth and twentieth centuries. There is a chapel, by no means a necessity by the 1920s, though this quickly took on the character of a memorial. There are also features that were, at the time of construction, very advanced: an electricity generator, set below the ramparts on the River Teign, and servants' quarters that were nothing short of palatial.

Drewe was an enlightened employer. A devoutly Christian man, he felt the sense of obligation towards his servants that was the hallmark of a good aristocrat and, having succeeded in the world of commerce, was no doubt aware that happy employees work more readily. He said that he wanted them to have 'a full view of the gardens', a thing no Victorian employer would have permitted, since they might witness all manner of indiscretions on the part of their betters.

The kitchen and its storage facilities were very modern and highly efficient, with much use made of cool underground caves for keeping foodstuffs fresh. There were no cheerless attic rooms for servants at Castle Drogo. The butler's quarters, which visitors can now see, contain a pleasant fireplace, a telephone and a collection of gramophone records. Though the butler was the most senior servant, conditions for those lower down the scale were also comparatively luxurious. Even the hallboy, on the lowest rung of the ladder for a male employee, occupied a 'manservant's room' which compares very favourably with accommodation in any officer's mess or expensive boarding school. The servants had a separate staircase and their own 'wing' in the Castle's North Tower, but these were of the same materials as the rest of the building. Their rooms had access to light and fresh air and distant views, and they had a telephone box of their own. All this was complete and ready for use just as the house became a costly anachronism as well as a place of mourning.

Construction was considerably affected by the First World War, which meant the loss of virtually all the stonemasons working on the Castle, for some did not survive the conflict and others did not return to the area. Indeed building ceased entirely between 1917 and the end of the war. Another loss was that of Drewe's eldest son Adrian (1891–1917) on the Western Front. It was for him more than anyone else that the house had been intended. After his death, Julius Drewe found it difficult to retain enthusiasm for the project. He became wheelchair-bound in the years after the war, and was disheartened by the length of time the building took to finish, as well as by the fact that it cost three times the original budget. He and his wife were able to move into part of the building in 1927, and the Castle was thus his home for a few years before his death.

Without doubt, Castle Drogo would have attracted ridicule from the inhabitants of more established and traditional country seats throughout Devon and beyond. Drewe did not allow this to distract him. His house soon blended into the landscape, where it has become an easily recognized feature to this day. The Castle had its own salmon leap and the fishing was excellent. It also hosted meets of the local foxhounds. Once they had had the chance to experience both its hospitality and its traditional country pursuits, it is likely that even the most snobbish among its neighbours regarded the house more favourably.

Before it was finished, though, Castle Drogo began to experience the problems of houses that were centuries older. Drewe had insisted on having flat roofs so that all the views from the hilltop location could be enjoyed.

The roof was of concrete panels covered with asphalt and, when the panels expanded in changing weather, the asphalt cracked and the roof leaked. This became a major nuisance, and one that was never to be solved during the family's tenure. Similarly, the amount of electricity generated from the River Teign varied according to the weather. When it was windy the supply would drop and all the lights in the Castle would dim dramatically, something that must have heightened the tendency to gloom among the tall granite halls. There was a sense of Fonthill Abbey about this place – of a house too grand to live in, doomed to fall victim to its own pretensions. It is sad to think of a family of great wealth sitting in damp and semi-darkness in the new home to which they had devoted such care and expense.

It was occupied by them for less than forty years – effectively a single generation – before being offered by Julius Drewe's grandson Anthony to the Trust in 1973. Designed to look as if it had stood for a millennium, and intended to be a family seat for a few centuries, it had proved too much for them to handle a few decades later. Built by the twentieth century's greatest British vernacular architect, one whose name will forever be synonymous with country houses, Castle Drogo was a glorious, but fittingly impractical, epilogue to the era of the grand country seat.

With the outbreak of the Second World War in September 1939 the remaining vestiges of country-house life came to an end. The traditional features of this – the London Season, the weekend house parties, the shooting and hunting – could not go on as they had, and neither could the expectation that staff would always be there to ensure their smooth running. Unlike the previous war, when there was no conscription until two years into the conflict and male servants could linger in service without breaking the law, this time both males and females were compelled to report for war work or military service from the outset. The call-up for men began in 1938.

A number of country houses were destroyed as a result of requisitioning by the armed forces during the war. Not only were the interiors terribly altered and hacked about, but several burned to the ground as a result of carelessness – drunken soldiers or thrown-away cigarette ends could destroy the heritage of centuries. There were stories of panelling chopped up for use as kindling, and of American servicemen racing jeeps along the wide corridors of some houses.

When war broke out, houses all over the country were commandeered by the Government for a multitude of purposes. Some were used for training (Osterley Park in Middlesex became a school for the Home Guard). Wilton Park in Buckinghamshire was used both before and after 1945 as a re-education centre for high-ranking German officers. A wise owner knew not to wait for the Government to requisition his house, but to offer it first. If he did this you might hope to have some say in what was done with his property. The least popular option was to have it occupied by soldiers. A better fate was that it be used as offices, or perhaps a research centre, by some official body. The most well-judged solution was found by the Duke of Devonshire for his Derbyshire home, Chatsworth. He offered it to a girls' boarding school which was being evacuated from a more unbearable part of the country. They accepted and moved in. The Duke was well aware that, with his home full of schoolgirls, it would be entirely out of bounds to soldiers!

Perhaps the most famous country house used in wartime was Bletchley Park in Buckinghamshire. A Victorian mansion that had neither beauty nor history to commend it, it had been bought – and saved from demolition – by the Government well before war broke out. It became, unbeknown to locals, the Code and Cypher School and the place in which a community of boffins cracked the secret codes of the Germans, making a vastly significant contribution to winning the war. Because of their isolation, the secrecy provided by their comparative remoteness and the walls that often ring estates, and because they were big enough to house large groups of people (the members of the Women's Royal Naval Service who operated the computers at Bletchley Park slept in the stables, two of them occupying each horse's stall), country houses were seen as being ideal for a multitude of official purposes.

For the majority of owners after the war ended it would never again be possible to assemble staff, even on the reduced scale to which the past few decades had made them accustomed. There was too much choice for young people of both sexes in terms of other work, both during the conflict and in the climate of economic recovery that followed. Domestic service had been deeply unpopular after the First World War among precisely the class of young men and girls that had previously been its mainstay, and their successors in the 1940s similarly had no wish to be tied down by the long hours and lack of mobility that characterized servants' lives.

It was sometimes possible to attract staff with other forms of inducement: one Scottish owner of a house offered the chance to live rent-free in the lodge house at the gate, in return for the performance of a single domestic task – bringing him tea in bed each morning. Otherwise, the owners of houses learned to make do and, to their credit, adapted remarkably well to the new era. Technology would continue to make household work easier. The vacuum cleaner became increasingly common, and the washing machine put paid to the need even for a commercial laundry. To a very large extent the landowning families took a robust view of changed times and embraced the need for discomfort and economy as a sort of adventure, an attitude summed up in the popular cartoon of upper-class life in which the owners of a house sit in their damp and freezing drawing room with dogs on their laps. When one complains of cold, the wife replies laconically: 'Put on another dog.' Antiquated plumbing that makes peculiar noises (perhaps attributable to a family ghost!), leaking roofs, howling draughts and electric lights that go dim at intervals, are all greeted with rueful jokes and even affection.

Many houses passed out of private ownership and have found other and better uses as institutions of one sort or another. The isolation of country houses makes them suitable to become various types of hospital. Some become schools, or research institutes, or exhibition space (Finchcocks, a charming Queen Anne house in Kent, is a museum of musical instruments). Their grounds can often take on a life of their own as public attractions, as has been the case at Nymans, a house destroyed by fire, to leave only a romantic ruin surrounded by beautiful and highly popular gardens.

The story of the English country house is not, of course, all a matter of decline and misery. Since the 1950s more and more houses have opened to the public, though this is a mixed blessing. They can only do so if there is some reason for the public to be interested in them. If they have no noteworthy items left to show, or have no architectural merit, or are too far from main roads or centres of population, they are unlikely to thrive as tourist attractions. Before they can officially open they must, of course, be able to prove that they have made adequate provision for the health and safety of visitors and for the disabled. All this, as well as the need to set up and staff a tearoom in the stables, to print guide books and tea towels and postcards, and to pay the wages of local people to act as guides or waitresses (though a surprising amount of such work is done from straightforward goodwill by volunteers), can make the economics of opening to visitors seem self-defeating, at least initially.

Nevertheless, the rising value of property has helped, and with land for development always in demand it is sometimes possible to sell off odd corners of an estate to help with its upkeep. Alan Wyndham-Green, the bachelor owner of Godinton House in Kent, wished his house to be preserved for the public. With the nearby town of Ashford lapping at the edges of his park, he shrewdly sold off a corner of this, in the 1970s, as a means of paying for the rest, and created a trust that, following his death in 1996, has taken charge of Godinton and its contents.

Many houses can make additional income as wedding venues. A change in British law that allows marriages to be celebrated in premises other than churches and register offices has meant that the beautiful and historic surroundings offered by a country house can be used for this purpose. If the house in question has a chapel, so much the better. Otherwise a lawn for the marquee, and the library or the stables for the bar, can be all that is required. Other houses are active in promoting themselves as locations for photo shoots, film or television. Every country-house owner is aware of the publicity value of having his home appear as the setting for *Rebecca*, *The World of Wooster* or yet another remake of *Pride and Prejudice*. In some cases the publicity fallout will last for years, especially if a television series is repeated. Some of the biggest houses – Longleat and Woburn, for instance – have now had decades of experience in running parts of their estates as tourist attractions, overseen by professional appointees, and have nothing to learn when it comes to pleasing the public. Some landowners, of course, simply do not have financial worries on a scale large enough to threaten their homes. The Duke of Bedford, owner of Woburn Abbey, is also the owner of much of London's Bloomsbury district, for instance. The Duke of Westminster, proprietor of Eaton Hall in Cheshire, owns an even bigger slice of London real estate which includes most of Mayfair and Belgravia.

The season for opening a country house begins at Easter and ends in the autumn, but increasing numbers of properties have discovered that Christmas offers another lucrative opportunity to lure visitors through the gates. Such is the appeal of a grand rural house in the festive season that it is not difficult to create a suitable atmosphere. In some cases this is deliberately nostalgic – Rockingham Castle in Northamptonshire annually stages a Victorian/Edwardian Christmas, with dummy servants and family members in appropriate settings and costumes. Chatsworth, on the other hand, puts on a lavish decorative display that has nothing to do with the history or contents of the house. It is themed, in much the same way that the windows of department stores are at this time of year, and is highly popular.

The age is long past, in other words, in which to live in an English country house is an unalloyed pleasure. Such a life was relatively carefree until about the middle of the nineteenth century, but for most families it has been growing steadily more difficult ever since. For every generation it is a challenge to maintain this heritage, which can seem not so much a privilege as a millstone around their necks. What is often very obvious when listening to the owners talk about their homes, however, is the affection they feel for them. To grow up knowing that, for generations and centuries past, your forebears have lived in these rooms, dined at this table, strolled in this garden, ridden from these stables, and that, equally, generations of servants spent their lives in service to your family, is a heady feeling indeed. It inspires determination to hang on to this heritage by any means possible and to do whatever you can to preserve it. No wonder the owners of these houses will so often put up a fight!

# 3

# UPSTAIRS

'I suppose no children so well born or so well placed ever cried so much or so justly.'
Lord Curzon (1859–1925), recalling his upbringing

Just as the public has notions of what a house should look like, so it has ideas – collected from a host of novels, films and television dramas – about the archetypal owner. English literature, as well as the visual media, have seen to it that the country landowner is a stock figure in the national imagination. As presented by the twentieth-century author or dramatist, the titled owner of an estate should be either peppery and irascible or, more commonly, amiable, bumbling, vague, modest, inoffensive, somewhat scruffy and – virtually compulsory – eccentric. The perfect example is the obsessively pig-breeding Lord Emsworth in P. G. Wodehouse's

*Blandings* chronicles. A real-life personification of this fictional figure was the 8th Duke of Bedford, the first member of the high aristocracy to open his house – Woburn Abbey – to the public on a commercial basis. One of those grandees who dressed casually to the extent of being unrecognizable as a member of the upper class, he was, according to his son, sometimes spotted by visitors sitting on a bench in the grounds. Mistaking him for a tramp, some shared their sandwiches with him. He was certainly not the only member of his class to avoid a showy appearance, for there is truth in the oft-repeated story of landowners who gave their new tweed suits to their gamekeepers to 'wear in', until they looked and felt comfortable enough to put on themselves. Today that essential garment of the English country gentleman, the Barbour jacket, is regarded as an embarrassment to its wearer if it looks new, and some will go to great lengths – such as putting it for days in the bottom of a dog-basket – to give it a suitably old and shabby appearance.

There are other stereotypes that are summoned up by the image of the country house. The mistress may well be a forceful, formidable personality, bristling with eccentricities of her own. The daughter is traditionally headstrong, either because she has always been spoiled or because she is trying to get some fun out of life before being married off to an uninteresting and unsuitable older man. The son and heir may be a wastrel, the despair of his parents, but he is often charming nonetheless. The most important family member is frequently the owner's mother – the dowager. Having been the wife of the house's previous owner (since his death she has been banished to a 'dower house' on the estate), she can be relied upon to criticize everything about the running or decorating of her former home, and to make her daughter-in-law's life a misery. Such is the power of this personage that the word 'dowager' has come into general use to describe any elderly and genteel lady who is firm in her views. The Dowager Countess of Grantham, played by Maggie Smith in *Downton Abbey*, follows in a tradition that goes back at least as far as Lady Bracknell in *The Importance of Being Earnest*.

While to our way of thinking upper-class people living on country estates in the Victorian and Edwardian eras seem to have been idle for much of their time, we must remember that they thought of themselves as very busy. Not, of course, compared to their servants or the workers on their estates, and not in the sense that their descendants are today, juggling jobs and commuting. Nevertheless even for women, who had very little chance to do anything useful, the days could be full. The elaborate system of calling on other equally unoccupied women, or upon local worthies, occupied a surprising amount of time. So did the 'good works' that were such a significant part of local charity at that time. Some instances were of vital importance, others a matter of whim. One fictional example can be seen in Benjamin Britten's opera *Albert Herring*, set in Edwardian East Anglia. The story begins with a visit by the vicar to the home of the formidable Lady Billows, the occupant of the 'big house'. She is in the habit of rewarding virtue among local maidens with an annual gift of money and with the title of May Queen, bestowed by her at the village fete. It is the vicar's task to select those eligible and recommend the winner. The plot hinges on the fact that no suitably virtuous young woman can be found, and in a break with precedent a man – Albert Herring, a delivery boy for the local grocer – is chosen as meeting the requirements of good behaviour. Intoxicated by his triumph, he spends his winnings getting intoxicated in another sense, and loses any claim to virtue. In the character of Lady Billows – as given to snorts of outrage as any gin-drinking colonel – gentle fun is poked at a character that had, and continues to have, real-life counterparts everywhere.

To some modern sensibilities the notion of an aristocrat rewarding the behaviour of others may seem risible. It did not seem that way to people at the time. She was presumably wealthy, they were not. If she was willing to part with money, they were willing to accept it. Before the age of media celebrity in which we live, it was the local aristocracy that provided 'celebrity' and brought glamour to local events, in the way that the Royal Family still does. The attractive young wife of the heir to an estate – a duchess or marchioness or countess – could attract a crowd to the opening of a church fete and be greeted with polite applause. Her beauty and her clothes would be admired, her utterances repeated afterwards. In a small town today the Christmas lights would be switched on by a television personality (probably one who is appearing in pantomime at a nearby theatre). It was not the equivalent of such people – actresses and music-hall stars – who performed this sort of task in the years before 1914, but some titled personage (or their attractive daughter) who lived in the area. It is worth remembering, too, that these people were not necessarily unknown outside the place in which they lived. There were, from late Victorian times onward, a host of illustrated papers or magazines in which they featured. *The Sketch* became the most popular, joining the already-existing *Illustrated London News.* These papers covered, as a matter of course, the events of the Season and the gatherings of the rich and titled. They published photographs of young women as they 'came out'. (*Country Life*, with its frontispiece portrait of a young woman about to be married, continues this tradition.) Their clothes would be admired by shop-girls; the announcement of their engagement would be greeted by readers with envy or sneers, depending on whether or not the fiancé was handsome. Though coverage of them was always respectful, they were part of popular culture in a way that is no longer the case. The public would often know the names of younger sons or elder daughters in the great families, and would follow the doings of 'black sheep' (in Evelyn Waugh's *Brideshead Revisited* the appearance of Sebastian Flyte in front of a magistrate, and the resulting headline 'Marqui' Son Unused to Wine', causes widespread hilarity) with the same amusement that is nowadays given to gossip about film stars and pop singers. Something of this is still apparent in the celebrity magazines of today – *OK* and *Hello!* – and, in the same manner, Victorian housewives and female workers would look through *The Sketch* and dream of being able to dress like the women on its pages. Instead of covering movie premieres, the illustrated press would send photographers to Monte Carlo to take pictures showing the season's fashions worn by expatriate British ladies as they walked on the promenade.

Aristocracy continues to reward endeavour and to assist the local community, and even in an egalitarian age such gestures are both useful and appreciated. The Duke of Northumberland maintains a Prize Fund to which charities can apply for grants. The estate office at Alnwick Castle also gives work experience, or internships, to young people. The notion of good works by local gentry – no doubt derided by some as 'paternalism' – is unlikely to die out completely.

On the whole it is true to say that families who had lived for generations in the same house or the same area took an interest in the local people. Whatever some may think of such 'paternalism' or of the notion of noblesse oblige, there can be no question that it brought benefits to the community. The support of local charities was one of the principal functions of the lady of the house, assisted by whichever daughters or sisters were to hand. Alms houses are still to be found in numerous towns and villages, built and maintained by the lord of the manor for the benefit of the local aged, no doubt including his own former servants. Remembering that, until the advent of the National Health Service in the mid-twentieth century, there were no public hospitals and that all of them were thus private foundations, either set up by wealthy individuals or by subscription, it is important to note that many cottage hospitals were the gift of local families, who maintained a benevolent interest in them. There were other benefits conferred on the local people too. One example was the owner of the beautiful Montacute House in Somerset, W. R. Phelips, who was responsible for installing piped water, mains gas and a modern sewage system in the nearby village.

We should not underestimate the extent to which the presence of an ancestral family in an area could benefit even those who had no personal connection with them or their house.

The milestones in the lives of the landowning family were often celebrated throughout the neighbourhood, usually with the help of funds or provisions sent down from the house. It was common practice for the tenants on the estate to make a presentation – paid for by a collection among them – to the eldest son (if not his brothers as well) when he reached his majority. When he married, the local community would decorate the streets with flowers, bunting and messages of loyalty. The Harpur-Crewes, owners of Calke Abbey in Derbyshire, had just such a relationship with their neighbours, tenants and employees. When Sir Vauncey Harpur-Crewe was married in 1876, the town of Melbourne erected a large sign that read: 'Welcome. Long Life and Happiness' (an arch bearing this sort of greeting was more usual). The young couple, as they travelled to Calke from their wedding, were cheered by enthusiastic crowds and their carriage escorted by mounted yeomanry in plumed helmets. When their son reached the age of twenty-one in 1901, he was presented with an elaborate illuminated address by his father's tenants. It bore his picture and the family coat of arms, and had a decorative border that showed views of the estate. When the heir to the Earl of Warwick, Guy Greville, attained his majority, the celebrations included the issuing of drink to the tenantry. An immense iron pot is among the artefacts that visitors to Warwick Castle can still see. A note beside it was written by a Victorian servant: 'I myself have seen this punch bowl filled four times when the present Earl came of age. It holds 18 gallons of Brandy 18 gallons of rum 100 gallons of water lemons & sugar in proportion. Jan 11th, 1872.'

A common perception of upper-class British children of this era is that they were unloved and kept at arm's length by their parents. Confined to nurseries and schoolrooms high above the main floors of the houses they could be forgotten except on special occasions, their upbringing and education left in the hands of specialist servants who came to know the children better – and received more devotion from them – than their mothers and fathers. This was by no means a universal attitude, however, and there is much evidence of indulgent, affectionate parents. There were aristocratic houses in which the children dined not in a distant nursery but at the family table, and whose mothers and fathers played games or read to them, but too many memoirs bear out the image of cold indifference for the image to be dismissed as untypical. A significant number of upper-class children, many of whom went on to do important things, appear to have grown up remote from the love or guidance of their elders.

While we are often surprised and even outraged to hear of such treatment of children by their nearest relatives, it would help if we tried to understand something of the perspective from which parenthood was approached by men and women of this class (and for that matter other classes) at this time. Childbirth was unavoidable for upper-class women charged with producing an heir. The Victorian aristocracy tended toward large numbers of children for the same reason that poorer families did: because it was likely that illness or accident would cause the loss of some before they reached adulthood. Large broods were, in any case, the fashion. Queen Victoria had nine children, and Society followed her example. For a delivery in 1859 she used chloroform to ease the process. This had been a risky, somewhat experimental procedure at the time, but its success in the case of Her Majesty made it at once widely popular, and easier births gave further impetus to an already existing tendency to produce numerous off-spring.

Once that duty had been performed there was no need to devote further time or trouble to children. In a world where servants were cheap there was no shortage of staff to take on the chores of motherhood. First the wet-nurse, then the nanny and the nurserymaids, then the tutor or governess. Children might also have a footman assigned to them.

Why were parents so uninterested in those who, after all, represented the future of their dynasty? It might have been reasonable to expect the opposite – that they would be constantly exhibited to visitors, studied to seek out family resemblances, their thoughts and utterances noted for evidence of precocity. In other words, why were these children of privilege not spoiled and doted upon as was more commonplace among the bourgeoisie? Why did they so often suffer neglect, or form closer relation-ships with servants than with their own flesh and blood?

One general reason for strict treatment of the young was that life was hard and preparation for it must fit them to face its challenges. Children of the servant class were perceived to have no need for luxury or pampering.

Let them instead become accustomed to plain living, plain food, modest ambitions. If their expectations were low, they could the more easily be contented with their lot. For those who lived in the nurseries of country houses, life must be hard for different reasons. They would inherit the good name of a great family. They must be worthy of it. If they were brought up in luxurious idleness, or with spoiled notions of their own importance (notions which many of them developed anyway), they could well bring disgrace upon the family through addiction to vice. More importantly, they must not develop extravagant ways that could endanger the family property and wealth. This concept is taken to an extreme by the author H. H. Munro ('Saki') in a short story called 'The Butter Dish'. An aristocratic infant expresses the desire to put his foot in a butter dish, presumably just for the sensation of feeling the stuff ooze between his toes. His governess is horrified, stating that should he be allowed to do this he would grow up to be spoiled, selfish and profligate, and would 'run through his fortune before he is thirty'. The urge, she says, should be beaten out of him forthwith. The story is, of course, humorous, but the point is serious. Those who are born to wealth and responsibility must learn at once that they cannot do as they like.

It was also commonplace that these were the children of parents whose marriages had been arranged and who were not personally fond of each other. Where there was little or no affection between husband and wife, there was unlikely to be warmth towards their offspring. The rising generation was left to the care of others who might, or might not, supply sympathy and affection.

Very often the parents had themselves been the product of similarly loveless families, and did not know how to treat children with anything but indifference, exasperation or bewilderment or ignorance.

Sometimes it was made clear to the children that parental dislike was personal and not general. Edith Sitwell recalled that: 'My parents were strangers to me from the moment of my birth.' This was because she was not beautiful, and appeared too brainy. Her father disliked any traits in his children that could be traced to his wife's family. Another intelligent and sensitive girl, Vita Sackville-West, had a similar experience. Her mother announced that she could hardly bear to look at her because she was so ugly.

A classic upper-class product was the young Winston Churchill, though his parents were untypical in that they were deeply fond of each other and had married for love. Their eldest son was devoted to both his parents, but they have gone down in history as aloof and unfeeling, uninterested in his company or his progress. This is probably something of an exaggeration, though they demonstrate just how preoccupied socially active parents could be. His father, Lord Randolph, was a Member of Parliament and was briefly Chancellor of the Exchequer, entirely focused on his career. Winston's mother, the American heiress Jenny Jerome, was one of Society's great beauties and a reputed lover of the Prince of Wales. She too was fully occupied with her role as hostess. The story avoids, however, becoming just another stereotypical anecdote, for Churchill's mother later on resoundingly compensated for any earlier indifference.

Though Lord Randolph died young, before his son's

ascent to success had begun, Lady Randolph became a hugely important figure in her son's life. It was she, through her wide-ranging and innumerable social contacts, who got her son gazetted to a socially smart regiment, who arranged the newspaper commissions that enabled Winston to work as a war correspondent while serving as an officer (something forbidden by regulations), and who enabled him to make the contacts that launched his career as a public speaker and politician. She did these things not out of a sense of duty but willingly, with enthusiasm. She and Winston were described, during the years that he was starting his career, as being more like brother and sister than mother and son. Many Victorian parents did not like children (the Queen herself despite having nine of them and a public image as a devoted mother, could not abide the sight of babies; she thought they looked like frogs). Once their young had grown up, parents might well behave very differently toward them.

Churchill's nurserymaid, Mrs Everest, was in his childhood the parent-figure whom he learned to love. She was idolized by him, and in turn took the greatest interest in his activities and his life. She was unceremoniously dismissed by his parents once her two charges had grown up (Winston's grandmother was apparently jealous of her influence over him), but he continued to visit her, and paid for flowers to adorn her grave after her death.

Even more significant was the influence of the nurserymaid who cared for Anthony Ashley-Cooper, who grew up to become 7th Earl of Shaftesbury. He was one of nine children. Ignored and openly disliked by his parents – he could never afterwards bring himself to feel the least affection for his mother – he received kindness only from an elderly servant who read Bible stories to him, and led him to the Christian faith that he was to combine with a political career. He was active in passing numerous pieces of legislation that improved conditions for the unfortunate, and indeed became the greatest British philanthropist of the nineteenth century – a man whose name is synonymous with goodness. So great was his impact on social welfare that the statue of Eros in Piccadilly Circus is a memorial to him. Such could be the result of a positive influence by a family servant.

Not all children were so fond of the women who ordered their lives in their earliest years. Lord Curzon and his siblings, growing up in the 1860s at Kedleston Hall in Derbyshire, were treated with outright savagery by their governess, Miss Paraman. He recalled that: '[S]he persecuted and beat us in the most cruel way and established over us a system of terrorism so complete that not one of us mustered up the courage to walk upstairs and tell our father or mother. She spanked us with her slipper, beat us with her brushes, tied us for long hours to chairs with our hands holding a pole or blackboard behind our backs, and shut us up in darkness.'

Though the experiences of children in the nursery or schoolroom of a country house would naturally vary, the notion of parents stiff and ill at ease with their own flesh and blood is one that is very widespread. Mutual awkwardness, and lack of subjects to talk about made contact between them an ordeal for both sides. Such visits were often a weekly appointment – in the

Carnarvon family they took place on Sunday afternoons at teatime – and were probably dreaded by parents as much as by children.

Where then did the notion originate that parents and children need not know each other? It dates back centuries, at least to the Middle Ages. Before the discovery by psychologists that childhood is an important time in which young people's characters are formed, it was seen simply as a training period in which they must learn the necessary life-skills as quickly and as quietly as possible. Aristocratic medieval parents sent their sons to the households of other nobles to take positions as pages and thus, in some sense, learn the workings of a great house through acting as a servant in it, performing menial jobs such as waiting upon table. This notion survived throughout the age of monarchies, for boys of noble birth continued to act as pages at Royal Courts. (In Germany, for instance, aristocratic young men in livery served the guests and then cleared the plates at palace banquets.)

The sense of inter-generational antipathy was allegedly expressed by King George V: 'My father was scared of his father, I was scared of my father, and I'm damned well going to see to it that my sons are scared of me.' This notion of parenthood is clearly one with which many people today would be uncomfortable, but it fitted the times in which these people lived. Parents were not supposed to be friends to their children. Their duty was to see that they were brought up properly. They themselves did not have the necessary skills to deal with childhood medical complaints or to see to the children's education, therefore they employed others to do these things – qualified and experienced nurses and nannies and teachers – sometimes the same people who had looked after them in their own childhoods. This might be seen as neglect, but from another perspective could be interpreted as devotion – obtaining the best available specialist care for them. And rather than wanting to witness their son's and daughter's first halting words or first steps, they would prefer to wait until their offspring were articulate and accomplished.

It is hard to understand the attitudes of past ages from the perspective of our own time, especially given the notion of the 'child-centred' upbringing that is taken for granted today. If the culture of the class and the generation to which you belong dictates that you behave in a certain way – if everyone around you who is in a similar situation follows a certain code of behaviour – you tend to do so too. If you are the mother of small children and your husband is the lord of the manor and the owner of an estate, you yourself will have a great deal to do. Your primary function is not to bring up your children but to make possible the smooth running of the home and the estate, oiling the wheels through the tasks you carry out. You are expected to spend a large percentage of your time writing or answering letters. You are to be at home to callers, to entertain your husband's friends or tenants, to visit the local sick and poor, to support local charities, open fetes, attend church on Sundays. If your husband is standing for, or sitting in, Parliament, and has an official career as well as his role in the locality of your home, you will have twice the entertaining and visiting to do.

You are also ultimately responsible for the servants.

You will sometimes be the one who interviews applicants for posts as maids or footmen or housekeepers. You are the one to whom they come with serious complaints. You discuss the day's tasks and their progress every day with the housekeeper. You plan the menus with the cook. Everyone expects you to do this. If you did not, you would be seen as failing in your duty. It is known, or assumed, that you have servants to deal with the upbringing of your children while you get on with the more important business of running your household. It is taken for granted that your children will not be very interesting until they are much older, and that until they have learned some basic social skills – until they can be shown to visitors without the danger that they will embarrass you and bring disgrace upon the family – they had better be kept out of sight. It is simply part of the culture to which you and everyone else belong that your children are best left in the hands of experts until such time as they have something to offer and can join the adult world.

For the same reason it will be entirely usual to send the boys away from home at what might seem a frighteningly young age. By the Edwardian era prep schools (at that time called 'private schools') junior boarding schools which prepared boys for entry to the great English public schools, at that time called 'private schools' – were taking pupils from the age of eight. At thirteen they would pass on to their senior schools. Not every boy followed this route. Delicate or highly strung sons might be educated at home, by a tutor who might be the local curate or, more commonly, a young man of intelligence but limited means who had recently grad-uated from university. There was a long and honourable tradition of such men undertaking to educate young gentlemen and aristocrats. To understand the life for which the country house served as backdrop, it would be useful perhaps to follow the young men from home to school or training and into the world beyond. Their professions and pursuits, their friendships and attitudes all explain something of the mysteries of upper-class British life.

If there was a naval or military tradition in the family, boys might go direct into the Service without passing through a public school first. Those destined for the Army could attend Sandhurst, the Royal Military College, from the age of about twelve in the early nineteenth century. This type of early start was especially true of the Navy, for, unlike the fashionable parts of the Army, service at sea required considerable technical expertise. Navigation and the other necessary skills took time to learn. Boys of twelve would be appointed Midshipmen and sent to sea to literally 'learn the ropes', so that by sixteen or eighteen they would be fully functioning officers. Queen Victoria's grandsons, Prince 'Eddy' and Prince George (later King George V), entered the Royal Navy as boys and undertook a three-year voyage around the world between 1879 and 1882 aboard HMS *Bacchante*. In 1903, when the Queen's former summer home at Osborne House on the Isle of Wight was turned into a naval training school for boys too young to go to the Naval College at Dartmouth, the practice continued of beginning the royal children's careers early by sending them there. Three of George V's own sons attended (the later Kings Edward VIII and George VI, as well as the Duke of Kent), as did their cousin, Lord Louis Mountbatten. Despite this heavy patronage of the Navy by the Royal Family, and despite its undoubted prestige as the world's greatest maritime force (a status it maintained until the Second World War), it was never as popular with the upper class as the Army, and neither would the Royal Air Force be, once that was established in 1918.

The sons of the aristocracy, as a general rule, were not educated at home like their counterparts in some other countries. Nor, by the nineteenth century, were they attending local grammar schools where they would share a bench with the sons of local tradesmen. England and Scotland did not have a state school system until the 1870s, and by that time private schools had had centuries in which to dominate public awareness and to accumulate prestige. Such schools dated, in many cases, from the Middle Ages, and had been founded for entirely different reasons. They were originally for the poor, and for the training of priests. This was the motive behind the first of them, Winchester College, founded in 1382. Such a school provided free education for a set number of scholars, but within a few generations these had been joined by other, wealthier, boys who came to the school to take advantage of the excellent teaching it offered. They lived outside the buildings, and paid fees to attend. At Winchester such pupils are still called Commoners. At Eton they are Oppidans ('townsmen'). Gradually they began to outnumber the scholars, and also to change and to dominate the institutions.

It is difficult to overstate the extent to which these schools formed a basis for the rest of their pupils' lives.

Schools would attract the fierce loyalty of particular families which would send their sons for generations (the record for some such families is now reaching close to 300 years), as can be seen by a glance at the names carved on the panelling in many ancient form rooms. Loyalty might be usual but it need not be absolute, and many aristocratic families have had members at both Eton and Harrow. The Dukes of Marlborough began attending Eton in 1722, yet in the 1890s when one family member, Winston Churchill, was sent to Harrow instead. The reason was that his health was delicate, and they felt a hilltop location (Harrow is known colloquially as 'The Hill') would suit him better than the damp vapours of the Thames Valley where the rival school was situated. Churchill's younger brother joined him at Harrow, but his son would attend Eton.

Within their parameters these schools were surprisingly democratic. However aloof they might seem to those outside, inside their community the titled and the most well-born were not granted any particular favours. The popularity of a boy would depend on an outgoing nature, a sense of humour, skill at games or in his studies (probably in that order). Titles were so common among the names on the School List that a holder of one could not expect to stand out, and he would be subject as a junior boy to the same obligations as all other pupils of his age.

Much is written about the English school system of 'fagging', by which the youngest boys in a school were obliged to run errands for the oldest, and to prepare their tea as well as some other meals – brewing the stuff itself, making toast, boiling or frying eggs. This ritual did not necessarily mean that only basic skills were needed: one boy at Eton in the 1850s, Sir Francis Burnand, was required by his fag-master to get up at six o'clock each morning to prepare a breakfast that included coffee, toast and grilled chicken, and in consequence became an expert in preparing all these things.

This custom, now extinct (Eton had abolished all forms of fagging by 1980), was often cited as evidence of barbarity and institutionalized bullying in schools. The zealots who criticized it would have found that most of those involved did not mind, and indeed learned some valuable basic culinary skills as a result. It had another, more important, side effect, unintended at first but definitely worth remembering: it meant that no matter how wealthy a boy or how many servants he might have to do his bidding at home, he too would learn to take commands and to perform menial tasks. He would have the chance to see life as it were from the lowest level, and might gain a new perspective on and sympathy with his own employees as a result. Similar practices occurred among the youngest cadets in the Royal Navy, and indeed in any community of young men who were making their way through a hierarchical period of training. Adolescents and young men of the lower social classes would be undergoing similar rites of passage – occupying menial and humiliating positions from which they gradually but steadily earned promotion and acceptance – in their roles as apprentices and office-boys. It was simply the way that things were done, and those who eventually reached the top could enjoy their triumph the more for knowing that they had so thoroughly earned it.

The dream of countless wealthy Britons was to own a house like this, a place of historic beauty surrounded by a landscape of park and pasture. An entire, well-defined lifestyle came with such houses. This one was Heanton Satchville in Devon, the home of the Clintons. They were created barons in 1298, making them one of England's oldest aristocratic families.

Supply of country houses could not meet demand and the Victorians, who acquired vast wealth from commerce and industry, therefore built more of them than any previous era. Buildings were usually designed to look centuries old, implying long pedigree. The one seen here harks back to the Georgians of a hundred years earlier.

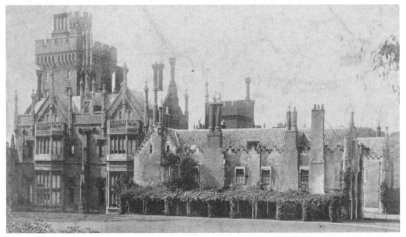

An eclectic example of the 'tudorbethan' style, based on English domestic architecture of the sixteenth century. In this case, the left-hand side seems grafted onto an earlier house, seen at right. Sometimes the client's needs, and the architect's vision, could produce catastrophic results. As tastes changed, a surprising number of such houses were abandoned or demolished.

No other people brought the art of gracious rural living to such a pitch as the British. The combination of house, gardens, sporting events and social ritual created a way of life that was envied, and emulated, throughout the world – and which was deliberately transplanted by the British themselves throughout their empire. Afternoon tea, taken informally on the lawn, was the epitome of this world.

Hunting demanded skill and daring, and had been the archetypal sport of the country gentleman for centuries. Here a hunt meets at the local 'big house' in 1872. They could have stepped straight from the pages of a novel by R.S. Surtees, a satirist who brilliantly lampooned the ways of the Victorian hunting set.

Every country house had a stable-block, built around a yard and often architecturally imposing. The clock was to keep servants punctual. The horses' stalls and the carriages were on the ground floor. Above lived the coachmen, grooms and stable-boys who looked after them. They, and their families, formed a small community distinct from other domestic staff.

The coachman, an experienced professional, was an important member of any country house staff, yet he spent much of his time on trivial errands – fetching guests from the railway station, taking his mistress shopping or on local visits, and perhaps merely driving his employer's children round the park to give them fresh air.

Girls typically entered service in their early teens but before starting had to buy their own uniforms, and it took about two years to save the necessary sum. Maids were almost always photographed in the black dresses (their best garments) which they wore in the afternoons to serve.

In the mornings, they looked rather different. They wore print dresses for cleaning the house, a series of chores that occupied the first half of the day. Servants were very seldom allowed access to the gardens, and their rooms were often positioned so they could not even see them. This picture was probably taken while their employers were away for the Season and greater freedom was possible.

Departure to boarding school had considerable advantages for young upper-class boys. Once they had negotiated the pitfalls of being at the bottom of a hierarchy and grown used to the discipline, they would make friends with other young men of similar background. It meant that, no matter where in the United Kingdom the boys' families lived, they would have grown up with those in their age group who shared their life experiences, tastes and background. They would cement these friendships through common experiences. It is summed up in a verse from what is perhaps the world's most well-known school song, composed in 1872 and sung at Harrow, one of the greatest of the English public schools:

> *O, the great days, in the distance enchanted*
> *Days of fresh air in the rain and the sun,*
> *How we rejoiced as we struggled and panted –*
> *Hardly believable, forty years on!*
> *How we discoursed on them, one with another,*
> *Auguring triumph, or balancing fate,*
> *Loved the ally with the heart of a brother,*
> *Hated the foe with a playing at hate!*

The schools taught conformity and responsibility. They supposedly instilled a taste for over-boiled vegetables and solid puddings —the 'nursery food' for which Britain was long notorious. Above all, they fostered organised games cricket, rowing and various types of football – creating a cult of the athlete the like of which had not been seen since Ancient Greece. Games taught courage, resourcefulness, teamwork, stoicism, modesty in victory and graciousness in defeat. Their beneficial effect on the British character and on the wider world cannot be measured.

Schools were run, from early on, by a monitorial system. In other words, older boys were charged with keeping the younger ones in order and ensuring that discipline was maintained. Such schoolboy officials had been stipulated in the charter with which Harrow School was founded. In some cases this system evolved or was adopted by headmasters of other schools who admired it. Sometimes the officials were called monitors, otherwise prefects from the Latin *praepostor*. The point was that they learned to exercise command, to help run the small universe in which they lived, to practise leadership. It would be easy to consider them merely bullies, and there can be no denying that bullying was rife, but as the century went on and the system became more structured and more supervised – once those boys in authority were made fully answerable to those above them – it worked well and promoted confident leadership. Those at the top of the school, their positions earned both by seniority and by skill at games or in study, were entitled to a number of privileges. At Rugby School they could in summer wear hats of plain instead of speckled straw. At Harrow they could carry a cane. At Eton the members of 'Pop', an elite and self-electing society founded in 1811 that fulfilled the prefectorial function, wore (as they still do) outrageously colourful silk waistcoats. This system of graded privilege in return for effort and service to the community was, once again, surprisingly democratic. The son of a duke could be passed over when prefects were selected in favour of a scholarship boy, if the latter were better at games or a more popular personality.

Such was the 'bonding' created by the shared experience of these schools – a thing that foreigners either tend to underestimate or simply fail to understand – that former pupils would be established for life with influential friends. Friendships were strengthened by the English cult of competitive games, something that transferred across the Atlantic and took root among American colleges but which failed to make the same headway on the Continent. To a very considerable extent, these boys married each other's sisters, perpetuating the same sense of exclusiveness – though at the same time absorbing suitable new blood – that has kept the aristocracy a powerful element in British society despite the advance of democracy and meritocracy. The boys whom they met at school would form the core of their circle of friends throughout life. They would meet each other constantly over the years and the decades ahead – at university, in regimental messes, in business, in the House of Lords or Commons, in gentlemen's clubs, and at a host of sporting and social events. They might become related by marriage, allied by political inclination, united by passion for sporting pastimes. Their education would give them an undoubted advantage when it came to positions at Court or in diplomacy and the higher reaches of government. Lord Curzon, the product of such a background, was appointed Viceroy of India in 1899 at the age of thirty. To celebrate this event he attended a dinner in London at which, on the back of the menu, were shown the names of all the previous Viceroys. The ones who had been – like Curzon – at Eton were printed in the school colour of pale blue. Only one or two names were in black. 'It was like the

P&O steamer,' Curzon remarked complacently, 'it [his school] was the only means to get there.'

The development of character became something more important than mere academic excellence in the upbringing of young Englishmen. The English upper class has never been known for its respect for intelligence, though it has produced writers and thinkers of genius, from the Earl of Pembroke (1566–1618) to the philosopher Bertrand Russell (who was also an Earl). Nevertheless, an all-round good character that was not given to too much reflection was regarded as the ideal, and this was summed up in a seminal passage in the novel *Tom Brown's Schooldays*, written in 1857 by Thomas Hughes (1822–96), a Christian socialist and MP. These words, spoken by the boy's father – a country squire and archetypal Englishman – as his son parts from him to go to Rugby School, perfectly express not only the expectations of many parents but also the more or less universal attitude of upper-class society towards the purpose of education:

> Shall I tell him to mind his work, and say he's sent to school to make himself a good scholar? But he isn't sent to school for that – at any rate not for that mainly. I don't care a straw for Greek particles, no more does his mother. If he'll only turn out a brave, helpful, truth-telling Englishman, and a gentleman, and a Christian, that's all I want.

In other words, decency and common sense were far more important characteristics than academic intelligence or book learning. The lessons of the playing field, and indeed the friendships formed there, were more important than the rote-learning that might fill a boy's mind with Greek and Latin. The Duke of Wellington was reputed to have said, in one of history's most used and most inaccurate quotations, that the Battle of Waterloo was won on the playing fields of Eton. This was nonsense, not least because when he was at the School in the 1780s the cult of organized games had not yet begun. The phrase has entered English mythology, however, because it so completely fits the image that both public schoolboys and society at large had of these places. They were 'character factories', seen as giving the best possible training to the young men who would go on to run both the United Kingdom and the wider British Empire.

To the British upper class, school was always a more important stage of education than university. To have attended a great public school was better than having a degree from an ancient university, because the schools were smaller and thus more exclusive, and because for many of the professions into which gentlemen went (such as agriculture or the Army) a degree was not necessary. Oxford and Cambridge Universities had been intended largely for the education of priests until the Reformation, and had nothing to do with the training or the values of the military aristocratic caste. Only from Elizabethan times did gentlemen's sons with secular careers in view begin to attend them in numbers, and the notion of these establishments as part of a gentleman's upbringing dates from that time. By the eighteenth century they had fallen into decay, and were wedded to practices that were viewed as outdated. They were therefore ignored by numbers of important families, for whom the Grand Tour was thought to provide a better education. An indication of the level to which they had sunk was given by the Earl of Chesterfield (1694–1773) who, when writing to his illegitimate son regarding the boy's career choices, suggested that he should enter academia: 'What do you think of being Greek professor at one of our universities? It is a very pretty sinecure, and requires very little knowledge (much less than, I hope, you have already) of that language.' The boy was sixteen at the time. Oxford and Cambridge could only be attended by young men who would swear allegiance to the Anglican Church, thus excluding those of non-conformist background. Members of the nobility, recognizable at once in court or quadrangle by the gold embroidered gowns they wore, were entitled to receive a Bachelor of Arts degree after two years, whether or not they did any work. Lord Byron, who entered Trinity College, Cambridge, in 1805, attended only one lecture during his university career, and spent much of his time in London. Because the college was not full and there were several empty rooms near to his, he was able to keep a pet bear (the regulations forbade the keeping of dogs, but said nothing about other animals). Even commoners could easily get through the oral exam necessary to attain the BA.

Families often developed a loyalty to specific colleges, just as they did to schools, sending their sons there for generation after generation. There was, however, another attitude in evidence. William Douglas-Home, younger brother of Alec (who was Foreign Secretary and Prime Minister), followed his brother to Eton and Oxford but, as he mentions in his memoirs, Alec went to Christ

Church (the grandest and most imposing college, so-cially as well as architecturally, in either university) while he himself was sent to New College. Christ Church, he explained, was regarded as an 'elder son's college' while younger siblings merited something less ostentatious.

Once there, there was no expectation that the young men should do any work, or indeed stay for the full academic course. This attitude had its origins partly in the fact that a degree had traditionally been so easy to buy or to obtain, partly that it was largely unnecessary, and partly in the fact that teaching staff, who were appointed for life to positions of prestige and comfort that they need do nothing to justify or earn, often had no interest in teaching or in the young undergraduates in their colleges. To an extent that Americans, with their meritocracy, would find difficult to understand, university was viewed as an interlude in which wealthy young men went hunting and played pranks and held supper parties. In Compton Mackenzie's novel *Sinister Street* (1913–14) the central character, Michael Fane, arrives at Oxford in the 1890s where the new undergraduates are told by the Master of their college: 'You have come to Oxford some of you to hunt foxes, some of you to wear very large and very unusual overcoats, some of you to row for your college and a few of you to work. But all of you have come to Oxford to remain English gentle-men.' A generation later Charles Ryder, the hero of another novel set at Oxford, Evelyn Waugh's *Brideshead Revisited*, says to his friend Sebastian Flyte: 'I think we should be tight [drunk] most of the time, don't you?' Flyte concurs.

Young men like these did not need a degree. Their futures were long-since planned, and the professions they went into would depend not on a degree diploma but on the contacts their families could mobilize. They would attain good positions because their fathers were acquainted with those who would employ them. Their backgrounds, homes, friends and interests were believed to be appropriate and therefore their integrity and their suitability could be guaranteed. Nobody pretended that matters were arranged otherwise. Nepotism of this sort was an accepted part of life. Until 1919 the Foreign Office recruited only young men who were personally known to the Foreign Secretary. As a system it worked surprisingly well and produced some very successful careers, which greatly benefited the country.

A particularly good example of the way the established order worked was Winston Churchill. Though not educated at university, he had a background as an army officer (which would have been considered just as good). He had brains and enterprise, but it was his father's political contacts and, much more importantly, his mother's manipulating of her extensive Society connections, that got his political career off to a good start.

For those who did attend university, the three years they spent on the Cam or Isis were mostly a chance to enjoy some frivolity before life became too serious. With the cult of games and the diversions of gambling and lethargy, there was enough to fill a young man's life without the tiresome need to work. There was plenty of time for enjoyment, and autobiographies dealing with this time are understandably filled with happy memories. John Galsworthy, chronicler of upper-middle-class

Victorian society, describes how one of his characters arrives at Cambridge from Eton in the 1860s, a time when the languid, upper-crust novels of William Whyte-Melville were all the rage. Modelling himself on the heroes of these, as did many young men of the time, he quickly suffers a fate similar to theirs:

> From continually reading about whiskered dandies, garbed to perfection and imperturbably stoical in debt, he had come to the conclusion that to be whiskered and unmoved by Fortune was quite the ultimate hope of existence. He passed imperceptibly into a fashionable set, and applied himself to the study of whist. He began to get into debt. It was easy, and 'the thing'. At the end of his first term he had spent double his allowance.

The young man in question is not a member of the aristocracy, he is the son of a wealthy merchant, but in order to be fashionable he apes the behaviour and the tastes of those around him who are more socially exalted. The aristocracy disdains 'trade', does not look upon those in commerce as gentlemen, and therefore does not regard it as a matter of honour to settle debts with them. His father, a self-made man to whom one's word is sacred, is baffled and disappointed on hearing of the debt and comes straight to Cambridge to settle it.

It is worth remembering that British attitudes to learning at this time were not the same as those to be found in the United States. In America the top drawer of society was made up of men quite different from their British counterparts. They were entrepreneurs, wealthy businessmen, and members of the learned professions of medicine and the law, which were widely respected as they required the longest study and the greatest measure of learning of any occupation.

In Britain, the elite have traditionally not needed book learning or academic qualifications. They could always employ clerks to do their writing – or even their thinking – for them. The aristocracy was a military, knightly caste, and the army officer was the nearest modern equivalent to a medieval knight. Other than this, the most suitable profession for an English gentleman was to farm his estate and, by serving in Parliament, help to govern the country. That is what the eldest sons of aristocratic families habitually did. Until the reform of the Parliamentary system began with the great Reform Act of 1832 it was common practice for aristocrats to have 'pocket boroughs' – parliamentary seats under their control – and to give these to sons or family friends. Some aristocratic boys at school and university already knew that, when they reached their majority, they would be given a seat in the House of Commons. Their younger brothers would go into the armed forces or the Civil or Diplomatic Service, or the Anglican Church – alternative ways of serving the nation.

For those who chose the Army, commissions in regiments were for sale. You could buy an officer's rank, the price varying considerably. 'Line regiments' – infantry units that were not part of the Sovereign's bodyguard – were affordable to the moderately wealthy. The cavalry cost far more, and the Guards regiments were astronomical. (The unfashionable branches of the Army, the artillery and engineers, which required technical knowledge and aptitude, did not sell commissions.) Prospective officers needed not only to satisfy their future comrades that they would fit in with the regiment's social and military ethos, but also that they would be able to afford it. They needed a private income several times larger than the salary they would be paid. An officer was expected to live fashionably, which meant the possession of horses and the playing of polo (this required a whole string of ponies), perhaps a carriage, expensive clothes, a mistress, and the full panoply of feasting and drinking and other vices.

A temptation that assails armies after a decisive victory is to live on past glory and not adapt to changing times. The British had claimed the lion's share of credit for the defeat of Napoleon at Waterloo (in fact, the last-minute arrival of the Prussians had been the decisive factor), and this had brought peace to Europe. There was no other prospective enemy in sight. The heyday of louche idleness among officers therefore took place in the years between 1815 and the Crimean War of 1853–6. Gambling was a besetting vice in some regiments. Young officers were expected to participate, but if any of them incurred debts he could not honour, he would be expected to resign his commission at once. The Crimean experience shook a number of these young men out of their complacent and hedonistic existence, for it was run with such incompetence, and resulted in such needless loss of life, that public and politicians alike were outraged. After extensive enquiries, committees and Bills in the Commons, the necessary restructuring took place. The 'Cardwell Reforms' of 1868–74 abolished the purchase of commissions and introduced a number of measures designed to ensure that efficiency would in future be considered before idle prestige. Nevertheless the connection between military service and social elitism was not seriously altered. There was still no question of officers being recruited from backgrounds other than the aristocracy or the gentry.

The expectation that only the well-born could, or would, serve as officers was common to all the old European powers. In many countries – France or Germany, for instance – it has disappeared today because of the cataclysmic changes undergone by those societies in the interim. In Britain, as is so often the case, no revolution has occurred to upset or replace the traditional order of things, and there is still a certain currency in the notion. A hundred years ago it was even more pronounced. Major General J. F. C. Fuller, who was a cadet at the Royal Military College in the 1890s, was to recall that: 'When I went to Sandhurst we were not taught to behave like gentlemen, because it never occurred to anyone that we could behave otherwise.' In parts of the British Army today this remains the case, and it is a system that works well.

That the British aristocracy had taken to the military profession with enthusiasm can be seen by the number of country houses that abound in family portraits of men in uniform. This is especially the case in Scotland, a nation that historically has been both poor (thus less able to support siblings in its great families) and warlike. Legendary Scottish regiments won fame throughout the world: the Black Watch, the Cameronians, the Seaforth Highlanders. Two in particular have had close connections with aristocratic families: the Argyll and Sutherland Highlanders has been virtually the personal regiment of the Dukes of Argyll, and the Gordon Highlanders were raised by members of the eponymous family. When in 1794 Britain faced invasion by the French, Jean, the famously beautiful wife of the 4th Duke of Gordon, rode through the local countryside and attended fairs dressed in regimental uniform, promising a kiss to any man who enlisted.

Because the Army has a regimental structure by which landowning families can serve in the infantry regiment of their county – these include 'The Buffs' (East Kent Regiment), the Suffolks, the Norfolks, the Northumberland Fusiliers, the King's Own Shropshire Light Infantry – the link between the aristocracy and the military world is thus a very close one. Some titled families raised their own entire units; the Percys, Dukes of Northumberland, formed the Percy Tenantry Volunteers in 1798 to defend their corner of England against the French. Almost exactly a century later, with the outbreak of the South African War or Second Boer War (1899–1902), the Scottish landowner Lord Lovat raised an auxiliary cavalry unit from among the employees on his estate and led it in action thousands of miles away on the African veldt. The Lovat Scouts, as the regiment was called, was no short-lived venture. It remained in existence as part of the British Army, and took part in both the First and Second World Wars.

Even where a family does not have a direct link of this sort with a regiment, it may well house, within its ancestral home, the regimental museum of a local unit. Military service did not have to be a full-time occupation. Throughout the 1790s volunteer regiments were raised across the country, and continued to exist thereafter. Cavalry was, as always, a more socially exalted branch of service than infantry, not least because officers need be able to afford their own horses, saddlery and uniforms, and the yeomanry regiment – a volunteer cavalry unit made up of farmers and country gentlemen – became an important part of upper-class social life within the counties. A local aristocrat, the natural leader of a district, was often appointed commanding officer. Members could design the uniform, and the result might be a riot of braid, frogging, feathers and tassels that looked like something from an operetta. One London unit, the Inns of Court and City Yeomanry, outfitted itself with such eye-catching splendour that the king, when inspecting them, said that they looked like 'the Devil's Own' (a title they have been proud to bear ever since). Their social events, for a regiment would usually have at least one annual ball, gave opportunities for flirtation as well as for the showing off of uniforms. The annual camp, a fortnight under canvas in some familiar landscape during the summer, gave both horses and men the chance for exercise outside the hunting season. An archetypal unit of this sort was the Queen's Own Oxfordshire Hussars. In the years before the Great War this was commanded by the Duke of Marlborough. His cousin, Winston Churchill, was a major in it and its camp was, on at least one occasion, held in the grounds of the Duke's home, Blenheim Palace.

This not only gives visitors to the house something else to look at but makes such a collection easier to maintain. The Duke of Rutland had for many years, at his home in Belvoir Castle, Leicestershire, the museum of the 17/21st Lancers. The Dukes of Northumberland have, within the walls of Alnwick Castle, the museum not only of their own Tenantry Volunteers but of the Royal Northumberland Fusiliers. The connection between the apparently peaceful farming of nearby land and fighting wars overseas is often an unexpectedly close one.

The Guards were – as they still are – the apogee of the British Army, the regiments with which the aristocracy are most closely associated. The two cavalry regiments within the Household Division, the Life Guards and the Horse Guards (or 'Blues and Royals'), are arguably the most aristocratic units of all, but the Foot Guards have an entirely similar ethos. In the nineteenth century there were three regiments: the Grenadier Guards (1656), the Coldstream Guards (1650) and the Scots Guards (1642). To these were added, in the twentieth century, the Irish Guards (1900) and Welsh Guards (1915), units that took on at once the same spirit of military excellence and social elitism that characterized their older counterparts. As with schools, so with regiments. The aristocracy supports them through generations and centuries, sending their sons to serve in succession. For a member of a good family this military interlude is a useful preparation for later life. Since the Cardwell Reforms officers have not been able to ignore the men under their care. They are expected to lead from the front and to earn the respect of their soldiers – to have professional as well as social qualifications for leadership. This may be the only time in the life of a landowning aristocrat that he deals on such an intimate level with people, en masse, of a class below his own. It gives him an easy confidence that will come in useful, years later, when his house is open to the public and he has to deal with them face to face.

The statement recorded by a common soldier, Rifle-man Harris, in 1808 while taking part in the Peninsular War, remained true throughout the nineteenth and twentieth centuries, and is still to be taken seriously today: 'I know from experience that in our army the men like best to be officered by gentlemen, men whose education has rendered them more kind in manners than your coarse officer, sprung from obscure origins and whose style is brutal and overbearing.' This is of course a generalization, because there is no guarantee that an officer of good background (and in this context 'educa-tion' is used in the sense of good manners, not learning) will not be brutal. Nevertheless there is a time-honoured relationship between aristocratic officers and their men.

Women of the middle class had, by the middle of the nineteenth century, been reduced to a largely decorative role. Professions were not open to them, and travel without a male escort was unusual. Ladies did not go to the country or the seaside or, often, even to the shops without a man to accompany them, either a person of their own class, a relative or a male servant. With few outlets for expending their energy and initiative, enter-prising women threw themselves into charity work or teaching, for the genteel end of that profession was one of the few that they could enter, and anyone, regardless of qualifications, could open a school or an academy. Ladies whose manners reflected gentility could make a living passing on their own refinement to younger generations, and this was an accepted occupation for the unmarried daughters of gentlemen.

As the century wore on, opportunities increased.

Formal education made a slow but definite beginning with the founding of colleges for women at Cambridge and Oxford (Girton, 1869 and Somerville, 1891) and the development of schools that were no longer based in the front parlours of genteel ladies but organized on the same basis as those for boys. Cheltenham Ladies' College was founded in 1854, St Leonard's in 1877, Roedean in 1891. While aristocratic girls continued to be educated by governesses, the daughters of the upper bourgeoisie now went away to school in the same way that their brothers did. Nevertheless, the same enforced idleness that had been the lot of almost all well-brought-up women in the middle decades of the century continued for those at the top level of society into the following one. The English upper class, as always, had little respect for intelligence or for academic achievement. Those who pioneered women's education were seen by society at large as bluestockings, man-haters, not-quite-respectable social and political radicals. They were not people with whom conservative parents wanted their daughters to mix. It took a long time for these schools and colleges to win the trust and the widespread patronage of the aristocracy, but by the 1920s schooling at home with a governess was the exception.

Women in general had by this time a wealth of new employment opportunities. The Great War had meant that many thousands of young females of good background had found useful and satisfying roles in war work and even military service – a thing unheard of in the past. Opportunities for secretarial work of various kinds had expanded, and it was no longer thought beneath the dignity of gentlewomen to work in this sphere. The same was true of shopkeeping, provided the business was discreet and appropriate (such as selling gowns or hats to others of the same class). The Great War, an experience undergone by the entire nation and in which sacrifices had been made more or less equally by all classes, had acted as a leveller and led to the rejection of old attitudes. The position of women had changed drastically. In the following decade they won the right to vote on the same terms as men. They smoked in public as a matter of course, they rode horses astride and drove motor cars of their own, and their clothing underwent the greatest revolution of all – for the first time since the Ancient Greeks and Romans, for the first time in well over a thousand years – women wore dresses that showed their legs. It was a new world.

The shops patronized by the aristocracy were mostly in the West End of London. As in many other spheres, there was often a long-established connection between a family and those who served them. Fathers would, when their sons were old enough to require suitable adult clothes, take them to be introduced to the family tailor, measured up and fitted. Tailors, as all the world knows, were centred on Savile Row, in the neighbourhood of Piccadilly and Bond Street. Shoes might come from Lobb's in St James's Street, and hats from Lock's a few doors farther down. This establishment, founded under another name in 1676, has furnished headgear to generations of gentlemen, aristocrats, and British and foreign royalty. Here in 1850 the Norfolk landowner William Coke put in an order for a type of hat he had designed himself. It was for wear by the gamekeepers on his estate.

Because the top hats worn by his men were constantly being knocked off by low branches, he wanted something that would withstand such accidents. The result was a narrow-brimmed black hat with a rounded crown. A prototype was made and, when he visited the shop, he tested the durability of this by putting it on the floor and stamping on it. The hat passed this test, and he ordered more of them. It has gone down in history as the 'bowler hat' because the first ones were made for Lock's by a family called Bowler. In the United States it is called a Derby (pronounced as spelled) because it was first popularized there by a visiting English aristocrat, Lord Derby. At Lock's it is still called by the title they gave it after the family name of its inventor: a Coke hat.

As with hats, so with much else. The aristocracy supported a whole range of specialist shops and craftsmen that supplied, bespoke, the things they used and wore. Many of these shops are still flourishing today: Ede & Ravenscroft, makers of robes for officers of state, universities and the legal profession, in 1689. Berry Brothers & Rudd, the wine merchants, was founded in 1698; Fortnum & Mason, the grocer's store on Piccadilly, first opened in 1707, its legendary hampers, filled with exotic refreshments, were taken by officers to the Crimean War, the Boer War, and the two World Wars; Purdey, makers of shotguns and sporting firearms, in 1814.

Ladies visiting London for a few days, or staying there for the Season, were less likely to visit a dressmaker than their male relatives were to go to a tailor. Many aristocratic ladies had very capable dressmakers at home, and they took their cue in clothing from Paris, not

London. Even the most famous 'dresser' of women during the nineteenth century, the Englishman Charles Frederick Worth, did business largely in Paris.

Ladies would nevertheless buy hats and gloves and accessories in Bond Street and Piccadilly, and would go to look for reading matter in the great lending libraries that existed in London at that time: Mudie's, Shoolbred's and the London Library. They could belong to these as 'country members', just as their husbands could have this same attachment to the gentlemen's clubs in Pall Mall or St James's Street. If they were of military background they could belong to the Army and Navy, the United Services or the 'In and Out' (the Naval and Military). If they were of an intellectual or ecclesiastical bent it would be the Athenaeum. The Travellers was for diplomats or adventurers, the Reform for those of liberal persuasion, the Garrick for those who liked to mix with writers and actors, the Carlton for conservatives, and the great triumvirate of St James's clubs, White's, Brooks's and Boodle's, for the top-drawer aristocracy and the old-established families. Among these institutions, which catered to the tastes and foibles of the upper class in the years before the Great War, casualties have been surprisingly light. The United Services Club has left its imposing premises in Pall mall (which are now occupied by the Institute of Directors, though all of its trophies and paintings remain in situ). Two of the lending libraries, Mudié's and Shoolbred's, once by-words for Edwardian respectability, have disappeared. Everything else is still there and still flourishing. Such is the continuity of British life.

# 4

# DOWNSTAIRS

'I am the son of a butler and a lady's maid – perhaps the happiest of all combinations, and to me the most beautiful thing in the world is a haughty, aristocratic house, with everyone kept in his place. [If] I were equal to your ladyship, where would be the pleasure to me? For it would be counterbalanced by the pain of feeling that [the footmen] Thomas and John were equal to me.'
Crichton the butler in J. M. Barrie's play
*The Admirable Crichton*, 1902

'His whole time being mine, he is not to leave home without permission, as each man is liable to be called in at night, in case of fire &c.'
Extract from servants' rules at Santry House, Co.
Dublin, 1864, written by the owner, Charles Domville

The ease and opulence of the leisured class was in stark contrast to the pace of life below stairs. The great majority of members of a country-house community were, of course, servants. They could outnumber their employers by as much as ten or twelve to one. The social and cultural attainments of the owners – the perfecting of this enviable lifestyle – were only made possible because there was a large, well-trained staff to clean the houses, feed and dress the occupants, transport them and assist with their sporting pastimes. One aristocrat, Lord Arran, was later to recall with guilt rather than nostalgia that: 'To live [the] life [of the upstairs folk] demanded that domestic servants should be slaves and contented with their slavery. It was only by slavery that the old regime could be carried on.' Were these people really the slaves we imagine? Their lives were unarguably hard. They worked very long hours and had little personal freedom, yet many were proud of the positions they held and grateful for the relative security they enjoyed. If they rose through the ranks to some senior position, they could wield a good deal of influence, make a lot of money and experience considerable 'job satisfaction'.

As the quotation above from J. M. Barrie's *The Admirable Crichton* suggests, however, domestics were not a single body, united by common tasks, common feeling and common purpose. They were either upper or lower servants. The inhabitants of a country house were therefore not neatly divided into 'upstairs' and 'downstairs'. There were three categories, not two. Though the gulf between upper and lower servants was not as wide as that between family and staff – after all, servants were usually of similar background, and those at the top of the hierarchy had earned their way there – there was remarkably little fellow feeling between the two levels.

Any resentment on the part of lower servants at the harshness of their lives might well be felt not towards the family upstairs but towards those who actually gave them their orders and who were in a position to bully them.

During the reigns of Queen Victoria and Edward VII almost everyone either had servants or had been one. Service was a system so widespread, so vital and so taken for granted that society seemed unthinkable without it. Even modest suburban homes could not have functioned without them. Clothes would not have been washed, dinners not cooked, parties not given, children not brought up. Things which house-owners, parents, married couples now do for themselves without a thought would have been considered impossible in those days.

Many thousands of servants were far from being the cowed drudges we might expect. Large numbers of them were well read, enterprising, keen to get on in their profession or to graduate to another. They often had musical ability, facility for languages, interest in the wider world. Many young people caught up in service dreamed of emigrating to newer countries in which the social order was less stifling. There were schemes to assist such emigrants, and thus a number of the most enterprising went overseas.

At its best, the relationship between them and their employers was one of mutual respect and interdependence. There was a positive side to being in service, though people's experiences were as different as the natures of those who employed or supervised them. Some would have been happy, others miserable, and others every shade in between. Few people are happy or contented all of the time in any case, so some servants would have enjoyed parts of their career but not all of it, or been happy in one household but not in others. Much that seems to us draconian, pointless or interference with personal freedom in fact made sense within the context of the place and the time. Even the notice quoted above, directed at those living in cottages on Mr Domville's estate, refers to the fact that service is a full-time occupation and that those who are in his employ must be available in emergencies, regardless of the hour. Fires were very common in country houses. If his were destroyed in this way, all the indoor servants would have lost their livelihood, if not their lives.

It is suggested in some costume dramas that there was a degree of confidence and warmth between masters and servants – that employers would now and again confide in their staff (who might even venture to ask why they looked troubled), or heed advice from them. These things are accepted by a present-day audience because they would be understandable behaviour today, but they would not have happened in the past. Once again, the makers of such programmes naturally want to play on the interaction between characters and are more concerned with creating drama than with historical accuracy. In reality it would have been profoundly embarrassing for any servant to be confided in, or spoken to with familiarity or friendliness, by a member of the family except in very rare circumstances: if they had recently suffered a bereavement they might receive condolences, but otherwise anything like camaraderie would have been considered highly improper. There were exceptions. Some servants' outspokenness was tolerated because of services rendered: the nanny who had brought up generations of a family might well be regarded with warmth by her charges once they grew up (as was Nanny Hawkins in *Brideshead Revisited*), and, having been a respected authority figure to her charges, retain their confidence thereafter, getting away with outspoken views that would not be tolerated from anyone else.

A well-known example of one such outspoken servant was Queen Victoria's Highlander, John Brown. A man of blunt opinions and charmless presence, and frequently drunk, he accompanied the Queen everywhere and came to deal with many of the arrangements for her general comfort. He had no qualms about telling Her Majesty, let alone her officials, what was best for her, and was cordially disliked by almost everyone in her entourage. Brown was an exceptional case, but otherwise to allow a servant such influence or familiarity was considered undignified and in very bad taste, and it was regarded by servants themselves as an insult to put them to such discomfort. The barrier between master and servant was necessary because the system would only work if everyone 'knew their place' and remained in it. Those downstairs desired this state of affairs as much as their employers above stairs.

In J. M. Barrie's *The Admirable Crichton*, the domestic staff hate and resent the efforts of their employer to treat them as equals. They do not feel so, and do not behave as if they are, and, significantly, they do not treat each other as equals. At Lord Loam's tea parties for his servants, when they enter or leave the drawing room they do so in strict order of seniority, and Fisher, maid to one of the Earl's daughters, is highly offended when he offers to refill the cup of the 'Tweenie' (whom she sneeringly dismisses as 'that kitchen wench') before her own, a breach of protocol that would never have happened in the servants' hall. The Earl, for all his efforts to ingratiate himself with the servants, does not understand this point, and neither do his family, who wonder why the maid is sulking. Meanwhile, the Earl's family are miserable. Floundering in conversation, one of them asks a servant, 'What sort of weather have you been having in the kitchen?'

Though it sounds a tired cliché, 'knowing one's place' had considerable advantages. To have strictly defined parameters of duty, behaviour and etiquette made it much easier to run a household smoothly. Servants not only expected but wanted their employers to treat them with aloofness. There is something of a parallel here with the code of conduct in the Army. An officer is expected to take an interest in his men, to know their names and backgrounds, but not to court their popularity or even approval. Though they will be polite to him there will never be overt friendliness, and indeed such a thing is entirely discouraged on the grounds that he may be asking them to risk their lives for him in the near future. Their social pleasures are taken separately, beyond his hearing, so that they can properly relax and criticize him if they wish (just as he can do with them). Though they will be respectful to his face, they do not want his company when off duty. So it was with a servants' hall.

In an era before there were the machines or the cleaning products that now exist, it required the work of dozens of hands – laborious, dirty, time-consuming toil

– simply to keep a house tidy. A comment made by an old farm labourer to the author Ronald Blythe about his profession is equally true of domestic servants: that whereas nowadays an employer will wear out one machine, in those days he would wear out several men. The work needed doing, and there was no other way to do it. Servants, like farm labourers and factory workers, were human machinery, and household jobs were more dirty and difficult than we can imagine. Where coal was the principal fuel, it was necessary to bring large amounts of it into the house, to store it, fetch it when it was needed, burn it and then deal with the considerable mess it left behind, largely in the form of black dust. There was nothing remarkable in this, it was how every household – not to mention entire transport systems of trains and ships – was run. The grates in which it had been used had to be cleaned every day, as did the other surfaces made dirty by it. The same was true of the oil used in lamps. Before the advent of non-stick pans or even piped-in hot water, the clearing up after the cooking and serving of meals could be a formidable undertaking – especially without the detergents we now have for washing dishes. Even the beating of carpets, a practice that is much more uncommon now that so many homes have them fitted, took a great deal of physical strength.

People – servants – got on with these tasks because there was no alternative. Dirt was unavoidable and its presence taken for granted, but it must be kept at bay through unremitting work and ceaseless routine. Clothing and fabrics and furniture were often better maintained than we are accustomed to now, and these, as well as the hard surfaces of floors and walls and stoves, required much attention. It was necessary to put much more effort into cleanliness, and the only way to achieve this was to employ a lot of physical labour. The servant class has largely disappeared not only because a more wealthy and educated population developed which preferred not to go into this profession, but also because the actual need for such a workforce is so much less than it was.

The number of persons in domestic service increased between the 1840s and the end of the century because country houses were being built at such a rate, but the profession remained predominantly female, as it would be until the end of the era of service. At the beginning of the nineteenth century there were seven women to every man in service, but by the 1870s the proportion had risen to eleven to one. A parlour maid was higher up the scale than a housemaid, for the latter undertook the heavy, and much dirtier, cleaning while the latter, who in the absence of footmen or butler might answer the door and be seen by visitors, dealt only with dusting and light chores.

Servants were paid only occasionally. They received wages quarterly, or even annually. They therefore might not have money in their hands for long months after starting in a post. They had, of course, no need of ready money during their ordinary working lives. They were not only fed every day but were entitled to supplies of beer, tea, sugar and meat. These, if they did not choose to consume them, could always be sold on. Because many who went into service had lived in poverty or at least noticeable simplicity beforehand, they would have been impressed by the amount of food in the kitchens of a big house. They would have eaten better there than they had ever done before, and were likely to have put on weight and developed a healthy colour despite the long hours and lack of adequate sleep.

There were also benefits in kind in terms of cast-off clothing. This might be especially beneficial to female domestics. Once again, it could be sold if they did not want it themselves.

The wages servants received varied according to where they lived, how wealthy their employers were, and what duties they performed. Those who were in service at a great house could expect not only better living conditions but higher pay than would be offered by suburban households. As domestic staff became rarer, though, the demand for them continued and wages rose. At the end of the nineteenth century they were up by almost 30 per cent, a colossal leap. Yet even with the lower wages of earlier in the century, servants were often paid in kind in a manner that was highly useful. The provision of beer was an important perk. Whether or not there was a brewhouse on the estate, there would be large quantities available at meals. It was weaker than it would be in a later age, so that more of it could be consumed. Because in many places water was not clean enough to drink, beer was used instead. The availability of alcohol negated the need for country footmen or butlers to go to pubs, as they habitually did in towns (the street-corner pubs in Mayfair and Belgravia were entirely for this class of customer, and gentlemen would not visit them). There were also tips left for the senior servants, which formed a significant part of their income. There was an etiquette to tipping, as there was to everything else. Lady guests gave to whichever maid had assisted them with their dressing and hairdressing. Gentlemen tipped the valet, but also the butler, the coachman and – if they had been shooting – the gamekeeper. They had in fact to pay every servant who had rendered them some particular, as opposed to general, service.

Throughout the Victorian and Edwardian eras, domestic service was the country's second-biggest employer of both men and women. Only agriculture involved more, and industry less. Even agriculture lost its edge as a result of the depression in farming. The aristocracy employed about one-fifth of the servant class. The rest were servants in middle-class families. The priorities for those with money to spend, and the status symbols they sought, were very different from our modern-day perspective. One of them was that any self-respecting family must have at least one person working for them, and that the more staff they employed, the higher was their prestige. Middle-class families would have a maid as a matter of course, though these did not live on the premises (suburban villas did not have servants' quarters included in their design). The maid to a country doctor's family, for instance, might arrive by bicycle each morning to serve breakfast, and depart once dinner had been washed up in the evening.

The Census of 1891 showed that more than 2,000,000 people were employed in domestic service. Of these, 100,000 were under the age of fifteen. Ten years later, the number was about the same, and statistics indicated the extent to which female domestic servants outnumbered men. Women numbered over three-quarters of the total:

1,690,686, over 40 per cent of the total female working population. Some of them were as young as ten, and their careers would commonly have begun at twelve or thirteen. They were essential to anyone wishing to live in cleanliness and comfort. Even a modest-sized home could not be kept clean or run efficiently without such help. In the case of a large house, or one in which a good deal of entertaining took place, it would be downright impossible to exist without an army of servants. As middle-class homes became smaller and were designed to be more easily manageable, servants vanished as a feature of domestic life and were to be found only in great households, as they still are. It was the great watershed of the 1914–18 war that finally brought about this change.

Servants gained respect from their own class in direct proportion to the position of their employer. This made sense, because the most important families could by definition afford the best service, the most elaborate liveries and carriages, and the homes in which the servants would be working would be the most splendid.

One surprising thing about servants was that, though many of them wore drab-coloured dresses, they were not blind to changes in fashion, or unable to follow them. During the crinoline craze in the century's middle decades even housemaids, on the little they earned, would wear those wide skirts whose iron frames could knock down everything in their paths. Cartoons of the time, in magazines such as *Punch* that found their readers among the servant-owning class, depict situations in which a maid is unable to kneel down to clean because of her voluminous skirts. Photographs of housekeepers, who wore ordinary dress rather than uniform, often show them in well-cut dresses with stylish bows, fashionably slim waists and elaborate sleeves (the 'leg-of-mutton' variety were especially popular in the 1890s), suggesting that housekeepers saw themselves as what they were: successful career women whose years of application had brought them to the top of a profession in which authority and organizational ability were essential – respected figures without whom an enterprise like a country house could not run smoothly. This was also true of male servants. Photographs of them off duty, or in ordinary clothes, will often show smart and stylish dress that suggests they saw themselves as belonging to a professional class and an honourable occupation.

For those who had domestic staff, there was considerable prestige to be gained from the number they possessed, and corresponding embarrassment if they did not have enough. Some of the grandest families had 'too many servants to count', according to one who married into the Grosvenor family, Dukes of Westminster, and it would certainly have been normal for the grandest families to have too many to know all their names. The Duke of Westminster himself would without question have been one such employer, since more than 300 people worked at his Cheshire house, Eaton Hall.

To us, much about a servant's life seems intolerable. But while there is no denying that it was a harsh and unrewarding life, we must not project into the past our twenty-first-century expectations. We have grown up in an age that encourages us to think we are entitled to personal fulfilment, education, satisfaction, leisure, material comfort, foreign travel and a wealth of entertainment, and that if we are not given these things we are being deprived of our rights. For those who did not have any such expectations, a life in service was often the norm. These people were a great deal tougher than we are now because their upbringing and conditioning and environment made them so. They had no opportunities to travel or to develop their minds. They knew they had to work in order to eat, and that there were worse means of earning a living than being a servant. They would, all of them, have known people – siblings, parents, uncles and aunts, friends – who had been in service already. They would have grown up knowing something of the work and the conditions and the things they would find there. If domestic service is what you expect, if it is what you have always been told you will do, if your whole short life is a preparation for it and if everyone you know is going into it as well, you must be at least a little accustomed to the thought of it.

There was something of a sense of solidarity between servants, if they were on the same level. Since millions were employed in similar tasks, the servant was a stock character in the Victorian world. They had their own set of attitudes, their own customs, even their own magazines. There was, as we have seen, a graded hierarchy, and the world of service encompassed everyone from the steward of a ducal household to the twelve-year-old orphan girl who did the domestic chores in a terraced house. A servant's experience depended on their position, on the work they did and on the people who employed them.

Some householders were aloof. Some were haughty. (Lord Curzon never bothered to learn names. He would

simply call out: 'You! Footman!' if he wanted something.) Others could be arrogant, exacting, vindictive,
lecherous. Many, however, were kind, thoughtful, solici-
tous, and loyal to those who served them. Ideally the
ethos of the English upper class included a sense of
responsibility for the welfare of those in their employ,
and the moral obligation to look after them when their
active careers were over. Some employers were of this
type, but there was no consistency. Being pleasant to
servants was not an inherited characteristic. One woman
in conversation with the author recalled a family who
had employed servants in her local area for generations:
'The old Earl – the one that died in the fifties – he was
hated, absolutely *hated*. He's still spoken of with hatred
around here. Then the son, he was very nice – very kind.
But the present one is just – horrible.'

In a house where the family were good employers, the
servants would naturally want to stay, and vacancies
seldom came up. In an unhappy environment the
opposite would be the case, though it might be difficult
to leave for another position without a 'character' or
reference. While they might spend a lifetime in the
service of a family, in other words, the conditions of
servants could change drastically, for better or worse,
when their employer died and was replaced by an heir,
or when their master married and a new mistress came
into the household. Sometimes a change in circumstance
might be caused by other factors: the servants at
Tedworth in Wiltshire were accustomed to an employer,
Charles Studd, who lived the life of an archetypal
country gentleman, farming and following the Turf.
Studd, indeed, was a somewhat raffish specimen of the

type. One day in the 1880s, however, he suddenly converted to evangelical Christianity as a result of attending a revival meeting. Within days he had sold his racehorses and converted the stables into a mission hall. He made his staff attend meetings there on Sundays, brought in speakers, and led the hymn-singing himself. When he travelled to London to attend services, he made a point of coming out halfway through to hold the carriage horses himself so that his coachman could go in and hear the rest. One of his servants later recalled that Studd would call out, if he encountered him about the estate: 'Giles, are you saved?' However eccentric this sudden change of behaviour may have seemed to some in the servants' hall, one hopes it made their master a kinder employer.

The house's owner and his family may have been kind or not, but the more junior servants, at least, would have had very little to do with them – if indeed they ever saw them at all. What would make a far more immediate difference to their morale would be their relationship with the 'Pugs' – the senior servants (who gained this nickname from the humourless, serious and self-important expression, characterized by a down-turned mouth like a pug-dog's, that they supposedly adopted to convey gravitas. It can often be seen in photographs of nineteenth-century servants.) It was these people who ruled the world in which maids and footman lived, and the lowliest servants actually worked for them – cleaning their clothes, making their beds and preparing their meals – rather than for the family upstairs. This was not a case of unearned privilege, for the Pugs had of course worked their way up the profession from bottom to top.

Entirely conscious of their own dignity, and demanding considerable deference from those below them, they could be more snobbish than those upstairs, and, if they were bad-tempered or tyrannical, could create an atmosphere of tension and even terror.

Most servants were female because there were far fewer other prospects open to women than to men, and the things for which servants were principally needed – cooking and cleaning – were traditionally female occupations. Domestic service was therefore by far the biggest employer of women right up to the outbreak of the Great War. Recruitment of servants was traditionally by word of mouth. A cartoon of the time by the artist Phil May depicts a young cockney slattern calling upon a middle-class housewife and saying: 'Please, mum, the lady what washes the steps for that woman which lives opposite ses as you wants a girl', and this was to a large extent how positions were found. In rural areas there were no agencies for employing domestics, though these came into being in towns in the late Victorian era and assumed increasing importance as servants became more difficult to find. Mostly, young men or girls were sought among the relatives of those already in service, for with the large families that were customary in the nineteenth century it was commonplace to have numerous brothers, sisters or cousins. Any of these who were approaching young adulthood could be recommended for a place, and it was often the mothers of girls who were most assiduous in looking out for opportunities for them. Settling their daughters in a good position was their final parental duty. It was of course necessary to get their children out of the home and into the world of employment as soon as possible. Apart from the need for their earnings it was a question of space. There were frequently other children arriving in the family, and no room at home for all of them. If a girl disliked her job and ran away, she might return home after even a day's absence and find that her bed had already been promised to a lodger.

Alternatively, girls already in a post would recommend others from their village, their town, their old class at school, who could be summoned to fill other vacancies. Employers and servants were both looking for each other, and it was not too difficult for them to meet. If personal recommendation were not effective, servants, both male and female, would attend the periodic hiring-fairs that were commonplace throughout Britain until a hundred years ago. These were mostly occasions at which agricultural labourers gathered to await offers of employment from farmers. Servants too would stand about the street or market place, conspicuously holding the tools of their trade, such as a broomstick, or the handled wooden boxes in which housemaids kept their brushes and other equipment, and wait to hear the question: 'Are you hired?'

The best background for servants was thought to be an upbringing in the country, so that even town houses recruited such young women for preference. Country people were seen as more wholesome, perhaps more innocent, more obedient and more hard-working. Although local people were very often employed, outsiders might be preferred. Those recruited from some distance away would have no contacts within the local community, and employers might only want such outsiders to serve them. Families knew full well that servants could be telling their secrets to friends and relations on their afternoon off, so young men and women with no connections nearby were preferable. These girls were also unlikely to have local followers. This phrase did not, as some assume, refer only to male admirers. Any friend or relative who would drop in to see them and sit gossiping in the kitchen was considered a nuisance. Before the advent of universal education, when illiteracy was more widespread, householders would also seek servants who could not read, so that they could leave correspondence or other documents lying around without it attracting curiosity. Most employees, however, were locals, because it was easier and more convenient to recruit them. In a rural area the children at the local school would know that, when they left, the big house was the likeliest source of work. Before the age of mass motor cars, and when transport in the countryside was expensive or infrequent, the option of travelling outside their home area did not exist. If they were taken on by the local landowner they might well be living on the premises or, when in the twentieth century the day servant became much more common, there would be a walk across the fields or a bicycle ride up the drive to get to work. One woman, whose mother went into service at a country house just after the First World War, recalled that: 'For people in this area there was nothing round here except to work for the Earl, either in his house or on his land.'

The essence of a good servant is a discreet and respectful demeanour, and this was instilled in them from the beginning. In rural areas where there were few other employment opportunities and in which the landowner, his house and his farms, provided the major source of livelihood, it was necessary to learn deference. This was something, in any case, that was ingrained in the rural populace. Until the 1920s – and certainly throughout the years up to the First World War – it was automatic for adults and children to touch their hats or curtsy, according to gender, whenever they saw in the village street the squire or a member of his family, and others who were deemed worthy of this respect received it too: traditionally the parson, the doctor and the schoolmaster.

At a higher level, the stewards and butlers and cooks and housekeepers – as well as the educated servants, the valets and ladies' maids – were of course drawn from all over the country or beyond. These might be recommended not by other servants but by other employers. They would otherwise either take advertisements in the 'Situations Wanted' columns of newspapers or would answer similar appeals for staff placed by employers. They were entitled to advertise in *The Times* on the basis that if they did not find work, they need not pay. Servants at this level would be interviewed not by a senior servant but by the man or woman for whom they would be working.

Ten was the average age at which to start domestic work for a girl, though by the end of Victoria's reign the school leaving age was raised to twelve, and this affected recruitment. The tasks she would be expected to perform, though numerous and difficult, required no more than basic knowledge and equipment, and therefore she could begin them while still a child. The vast majority of those who went into service worked not in the homes of the aristocracy but in the homes of the middle- and lower-middle class. Their employers would often be from backgrounds little better than their own, but such was the kudos – and the necessity – of having servants that these small households absorbed millions of such youngsters. Here a girl would be expected to clean floors and stoves, to scrub dishes, to look after children scarcely older than herself, to run errands, do washing and ironing. This was the world of the 'maid-of-all-work', who was, as her name suggests, a pitiable drudge and general dogsbody. This type of girl, frequently sent from the nearest orphanage or workhouse, was destined for a life that offered little hope of advancement. She had no companions of her own age, no company other than her employers, no time off, no guaranteed or regular wages, no prospect of learning useful skills and rising in her 'profession'. Her only alternative might well be to run away and go on the streets. To such girls as these, the life of a junior servant in a large and wealthy household would have seemed like paradise.

On the other hand, these girls could go straight into work, for they wore their everyday clothes. Those who sought positions in better households had to provide their own uniforms. This was no easy task, because there would be several of them required. Maids needed clothes for cleaning as well as for serving their employers. They needed caps and aprons, and even the array of brushes and other tools with which they would work. It took an average of two years to save the money to buy all of this, and the funds had to be raised by other work, such as child-minding. It might be that parents or other family members could supply some of the money or that a local lady, keen to help young women get a start in life, would oblige. It was owning this equipment that set a maid in a grand household apart from the thousands of humbler domestics.

A maid needed to have at least two dresses. One should be black, any others print. The former was for what might be termed 'public duties' in the afternoon, the latter for household cleaning in the mornings. She also needed several white aprons besides the starched cuffs and collars that adorned these outfits. The 'morning apron' was to wear during the heavy and dirty cleaning of floors and grates that occupied the first half of the day, and was made of hessian. The starched white apron that is more often associated with maids was for afternoon wear, and was worn with the black dress. We do not hear of this clothing being passed on second-hand, which would have been an entirely normal thing to do. The fact was that the clothes did not survive because they took such hard wearing, and employers would not have wanted to see a maid in shabby or ill-fitting clothing anyway. In London and every other large city there would be specialist shops for servants that could provide the entire assemblage of clothing – dresses, caps, aprons, shoes and stockings – together with advice on how to maintain them. The little wardrobe would be packed into a tin trunk, for this was the only piece of luggage a maid could take with her.

The aprons, and the caps that were worn with them, had to be spotless even if no one from upstairs was likely to see the girl. Washing and pressing them was therefore a frequent and time-consuming chore. The material given by mistresses to their maids at Christmas for making new dresses was in one sense a saving, but if they had not the necessary skill in dressmaking they would have to pay someone else to create the garment for them, and this would have to be done out of their wages.

Country-house servants were the aristocracy of their class, just as their employers might be in a more literal sense. If you were a girl of twelve or thirteen, employed as a maid-of-all-work by a titled family, away from home and cut off from everything you knew, you would have had good grounds for feeling sorry for yourself. Yet although you would work very long hours, although no one would pay you any attention – except when there was blame to throw around – and although your life was hard and cheerless, there was nevertheless much to look forward to, and to be thankful for. You might sleep in a tiny attic room, but would share it with only one other person instead of the numerous brothers and sisters there were at home. You would never have had so much space or comparative privacy. You would be earning a wage, and have your meals provided. You would be astonished by the quantity of food on offer and appalled by how much was thrown away, but could expect to look and feel healthier on this diet than ever before. In the evenings the food in the servants' hall would be the same as that eaten by the family upstairs, because it would consist of their leftovers – food that many members of your own class would not have had the chance to taste. Your working conditions would be considerably better than those of your schoolfriends who had gone into other domestic jobs (you at least would have the hallboy to help you carry heavy coal scuttles upstairs) or into more back-breaking labour in agriculture or down mines. Though you were worked hard, you would have precisely delineated tasks and, so long as you carried them out competently, you could look forward to advancing in due course up the service hierarchy.

As soon as you had learned the geography, the personalities and the rules of behaviour in the house, things would have started to get easier for you. The work would have been physically taxing but endurable, and with conditioning it would have been possible to pace yourself. Other servants, some of them recently in the same lowly position, could have offered commiseration, acceptance, comradeship – as well as tips on how to take short cuts with the work or to avoid antagonizing those in authority.

It is interesting to reflect that our imaginary young girl, aged about thirteen, would not be so far removed in her unhappiness from the son of the house, who at the same age would be starting at boarding school. At Eton and Harrow the boys did not sleep in dormitories but in single rooms, and those assigned to the most junior boys would have been the smallest and meanest – about the same size as those in a servants' corridor. There would be a similar sense of loneliness and of parting from all that was familiar. Though the hours of a schoolboy would not have been as long, and the work less strenuous, it is worth remembering that the 'fagging system' that was customary at English schools involved small boys in often menial domestic chores and that the failure to carry these out successfully could lead to bullying and punishment.

The severity of this life was sometimes extreme:

'privations that would have broken a cabin boy', as one veteran put it. Lord Holland, a fag at Eton in the 1820s, was disabled for life by having his hands burned because he was made to hold slices of bread over an open fire while making toast. Robert Gascoyne-Cecil, who as Lord Salisbury would serve as Prime Minister three times during the Victorian era, was so bullied at the same school that he wrote piteously – and vainly – to his father begging to be removed, and in later life avoided anyone whom he had known there. Conditions gradually improved during the nineteenth century and society in general became gentler, but any small boy could be a target for bullying. The humblest maid and the heir to the house might have had much in common.

In the meantime our scullery maid would have the camaraderie of the servants' hall and the company of other young people, the thought of the servants' dances and occasional outings to provide the brighter moments in life, and one day the chance to go home for an afternoon and show off her maid's dress and bring gifts of foodstuffs from the kitchen or fruit from the estate. By that time she would long since have learned the snobbish disdain of servants in a grand house for those who worked in places smaller than their own, or for employers who were poorer, less stylish or without titles, and everyone would be impressed by her sophistication.

She would be at the bottom of a ladder, but one that could lead to dizzying heights among what were sometimes called the 'top stair' – the senior servants. From learning the skills of service, she could progress to chambermaid – just as the hallboy could hope one day to be a footman or even an under-butler – positions that commanded respect within their class, and which included the outward glory of livery or a smart uniform as well as the prospect of getting tips from visitors. Beyond that, if you could somehow get the training and win the favour of an employer, there were specialist positions in which they would be trusted with the care of individual ladies or gentlemen – as dresser or valet – and these would enable you to travel extensively while accompanying their employer, though to secure such a position they would need a lot of personal qualities and qualifications. And at the pinnacle of a life of service there would be the posts of housekeeper or butler, almost unimaginably grand and far removed though these would seem.

They would quickly take on the snobbery that goes with life in a big house. Whatever your position below stairs, you would be part of something great and important, as far removed from the 'slavey' of the small household as a peacock from a crow. They would become vicariously proud of the splendour of their master's house, the elegance of their mistress's dresses, the magnificence of the liveried footmen and coachmen, even though none of these would deign to notice them – and the footmen, in particular, would not lift a finger to help carry heavy burdens up the stairs because they would consider it beneath them or have the excuse that they could not get their clothing dirty. Like all those who live in a close-knit community, united by a common purpose and common grievances, the household servants would look on everyone else as an outsider.

Should one wish to leave service, they would find your

training had made them highly suitable to work as a shop assistant, a steward on an ocean liner, or in a hotel or restaurant. Indeed if their employer was someone of high position, they might find yourself in great demand, to shed lustre on whatever enterprise or institution you joined next. By the time they had put a decade or more of service behind them, you would have a highly marketable range of experience and skill. This would be worth remembering, while they were scrubbing grates or blacking boots, early on a cold winter's morning.

The early Victorian era saw considerable changes in the physical surroundings of those who worked for the family. The servants' wing in many houses became larger, and the number of staff increased for a few decades, before numbers began their inexorable decline. For reasons already suggested, the employers of servants wanted to protect them from idleness and immorality – given that some of the girls and young men in their households were as young as thirteen, it is understandable that employers and senior servants should have seen themselves as acting *in loco parentis* – a situation that would be even more true today as a result of child-protection laws. To discourage temptation, the bedrooms of male and female staff were usually situated in entirely different parts of the house, with men in the basement and females in the attic. There might even, if the design of the house permitted, be separate staircases for the sexes.

It is worth noticing that this notion was starting to disappear before the century was over. By the 1890s servants were still separated by sex, if not as rigidly as before, but the accommodation planned for domestic staff in the new country houses then being built was much less obvious and not so large. The number of available servants was just beginning to decline, the number of part-time staff had increased, the introduction of labour-saving domestic devices was already beginning to be apparent. There simply was less need for doing things on the grand scale.

The segregation of staff made perfect sense to those who employed servants. Flirting and dalliance were a serious distraction from the work for which these men and women were being paid. They caused inattention and might, if a friendship was ended by a quarrel, create an unpleasant working atmosphere. The prospect of a servant 'getting into trouble' was a serious threat to the efficiency of a household as well as to the future of the woman concerned. Given the social stigma attached to unmarried pregnancy throughout the whole of this period, employers who kept their young maids from temptation were doing them a considerable kindness, whether the girls appreciated it or not.

As for the banning of 'followers', an attitude more common in Victorian times than later, this too was a wise precaution. Apart from suffering the same danger of visitors distracting girls who had much to do, why should householders allow unknown people into the servants' quarters of their home, where they would be within reach of temptation in the form of both wine and silverware? It was well-established practice for burglars and housebreakers to befriend impressionable maids and thus gain access. They might then either 'case the joint' and plan a robbery, or corrupt the girl into acting as accomplice and giving them a key. The most seemingly innocent questions about the household's routine could yield valuable information about when the owners were away or how many male servants there were. No mistress, in any case, wanted to find a strange man sitting by the servants' hall fireplace, or listen to obvious falsehoods about him being the maid's brother, or to know that the doings of herself and her family were being spoken about with outsiders. How much better to keep this danger completely at bay by banning all callers.

From the employer's point of view it made perfect sense to impose these regulations, yet young and attractive servant girls ran a very considerable risk of getting into trouble not only from the attentions of their 'followers' and fellow servants but also from members of their employer's own family. Any male inhabitant of the upstairs world could make advances to them, and these could not be rebuffed easily, for neither physical force – if they had sufficient strength – nor verbal rudeness could be used. Should a maid consent to the attentions of such a man and 'get into trouble', she would be sacked at once, without a 'character' and with the prospect of caring for an illegitimate child. Much has been made by writers of the double standards of employers, who overlooked their own sexual adventures yet expected their staff to be celibate, or who used young women for sexual gratification and then dismissed them when the consequences became apparent. Unfortunately this hypocritical behaviour was true of many.

To avoid this situation, young women went to subtle but inventive lengths. On weekdays they often did not see their employers, for they carried out their work before the family was up or after it had gone out. On Sundays, servants were expected to attend church, dressed in their best, off-duty clothes and thus looking as attractive as possible. Wise young women were careful to take trouble to disguise whatever beauty they might have. One, whose mother was in service to an Earl during the 1920s, recalled hearing that they pulled their hats down as far over their eyes as possible – the cloche hats then in vogue could hide much of the face – and that they rubbed starch into whatever hair was visible, to make it look grey. Similarly they whitened their cheeks to make themselves look paler. They no doubt walked with their heads down and avoided eye contact too. This would go on perhaps for years, until the arrival of middle age made genuine the appearance they had striven to use as a disguise.

Though many who were in service would form romantic friendships – after all, they were mixing every day with young people of the opposite sex – these could not become serious without complicating both work and life. Romance or marriage between servants was extremely rare in Victorian times; it was more common and more accepted by the reign of Edward VII, as servants became harder to keep contented and conditions improved, and by the inter-war period it was often considered convenient to have a husband and wife working in a household. They required less complicated accommodation and, settled in life, were less likely to leave a position at short notice.

As for the sons or husbands or uncles who might make nuisances of themselves with pretty servant girls, there was little that could be done about them. Maids would often protest: 'You're damned if you do and damned if you don't.' If they were caught, or got into trouble, they would be out at once. It was always their fault and not the man's, even though resisting his blandishments might get maids into just as much trouble. Rose Plummer, a tough East Ender, was a maid in the 1920s. Her striking looks led at least two men to make serious passes at her. One was the brother of the woman who employed her, then staying as a guest in her mistress's house. Though he never came close to indecent behaviour, his continued attentions were disconcerting to her and a nuisance. After a few days Rose was summoned to see her mistress. She expected to be given a dressing-down for something, but instead received 'the biggest surprise of my whole life'. The woman was actually embarrassed as she said: 'I want to apologize for the fact that you have been very shabbily treated by a member of my family. I'm so sorry you have been upset by it. It's disgraceful, and if there is anything I can do you must let me know.' The bothersome man was sent away shortly afterwards. This would not have been a common experience, however.

In a house without servant's wings, maids were traditionally in the attic. This was because the male staff lived in the basement and the two sexes needed to be kept as far apart as possible. The passageway off which they slept would often be guarded by the housekeeper's own quarters.

In the basement, the butler was in similarly close proximity to the male staff, with his pantry next to the wine cellar and the strong room where the plate was kept. The housekeeper's room – unlike the butler, she did

not sleep in her 'office' but used it only during the day –
was also in the basement. It was here, in the 'Pugs'
Parlour', that the senior servants dined. This was a
custom that, with variations according to different
households, was to be found all over Britain. At Welbeck
Abbey, home of the Duke of Portland, the senior
servants were known as the 'Upper Ten', and dined
separately each evening in the Steward's Dining Room.
All the other members of staff were known as the 'Lower
Five'. The seniors might take all courses in the Pugs'
Parlour, waited upon by their juniors, or might retire
there only to have port and cheese, in precisely the way
that the occupants of High Table still do at Oxford and
Cambridge colleges. They did not take all meals in this
manner, though. At other times they sat with the lower
servants, the cook and housekeeper at one end of the
table and the butler or the steward at the other, with the
juniors in between. Part of their function, after all, was
to supervise those under their authority. They would be
expected to steer the conversation, discourage flirting,
see that no one was volubly critical of their masters, and
set an example of good table manners.

   Given the general culture of servant-keeping, with its
long working hours and scarcity of free time, it may be
wondered why so many families seem to have been so
strict – unkind, even – to those who worked for them.
There was a general perception among those upstairs that
if they were indulgent, their servants would take
advantage. They had to be kept on a short rein and
prevented from becoming too comfortable, too idle, too
familiar, too complacent. There is logic in this. If they
were able to get away with insolence or even disrespect,

their employer's authority would be undermined, and
for the proper running of the household this could not
be allowed to happen. If the servants thought they could
succeed in doing less work, they would naturally try,
despite the fact that they were being paid for a full day's
service. If they were not kept constantly busy they might
be tempted to rifle their employer's belongings, pilfer
things, help themselves to the contents of the wine cellar.
They must be made accountable for how their time was
spent, and kept out of both trouble and temptation.

Servants, for their part, possessed a whole armoury of
weapons for getting back at their masters. They would
deliberately work slowly, fail to answer summons,
pretend not to have heard requests or the ringing of bells,
spill things or knock them over, affect to have misunder-
stood instructions, tell lies. A great deal of this would be
impossible to prove and difficult to punish. A famous
cartoon by George Cruikshank depicts four servants
lolling by the kitchen fire and smirking as a bell is rung
repeatedly to summon them. The caption reads: 'Oh, ah!
Let 'em ring again!' The more skilled the servant, the
more difficult perhaps to replace, the more they could
get away with. It might well be dangerous for a family
to annoy those who prepared and served its meals.

It is worth remembering that for some rural girls,
service was not a commitment for life but a sort of
domestic science training college. They went to work in
a house, for a period of two or three years, when they
were old enough to do so. This enabled them to perfect
the skills of cooking and cleaning, and perhaps child-
minding, that would be useful for running their own
homes. Their future husbands saw this as a rite of

passage, for it qualified them to be housewives. These young women may not have been officially allowed to have 'followers', but they often had in mind the young man who represented their future.

Though many servants thought of their work as a lifetime's career, they knew that their employment could come to an abrupt end. They had no security of employment, could be dismissed without warning for any one of numerous misdemeanours (though they would usually be given notice), and would have very little opportunity to defend themselves. 'Characters' – job references from previous employers – were all-important. The notion of the servant 'dismissed without a character', or sent away with a very bad one, is among the best-known clichés of the Victorian domestic world, but it need not always have been the disaster we imagine. Characters could easily be forged, in much the same way that resumés are today, and in any case a prospective employer could very often read between the lines and deduce that personal animosity lay behind an unfavour-able reference. It actually became illegal to give an unjustified negative reference to a servant (the fine was £20), but malice was hard to prove. It was also against the law for an employer, when writing a character reference, to conceal any misdemeanours. As Mrs Beeton put it with admirable clarity: 'It is not fair for one lady to recommend to another a servant she would not keep herself.' We must remember too that it was not always a case of employers dismissing and servants being made destitute. It was perfectly common for a servant to give notice if they heard of better prospects.

It was often difficult to climb the hierarchy within the

same household, and therefore servants expected to move from one place to another. Many were constantly on the lookout, as ambitious people tend to be, for better prospects. They might even be 'headhunted' by another employer who had been impressed by them while visiting. Though there were of course servants who remained in the same household all their lives, through loyalty, inertia or because their place of work was conveniently situated, it was far more common than we perhaps realize for members of domestic staffs to change their employer and to move around, especially by the Edwardian era when communications were better. The difficulty of keeping good servants is one of the recurring themes in the pages of that middle-class barometer, *Punch*. Employers were often disappointed by the lack of loyalty shown by servants whom they had trained, housed and – in their own view at least – treated like members of the family, only to have them flounce out of the door as soon as they had the chance. But servants, if they were proficient in their jobs, were aware of how much their skills were worth. They met other maids or footmen when visiting houses with their employers, and would constantly be comparing their wages and living conditions with those of their counterparts elsewhere. And they knew perfectly well that the threat of departure would often cause their mistress or master to raise their wages as an inducement for them to stay.

It is important to remember that, however much a Victorian house may have seemed a permanent community in which faces did not change, there was constant coming and going among servants. Though there were of course retainers who stayed for decades in the same post, these might be the exception rather than the rule, and the notion that a young person would enter the kitchens of the local big house at thirteen and still be there at fifty is by no means a valid one. Mobility was of course more limited for those at the bottom of the hierarchy. They had no marketable skills and, because they were not visible to the world of upstairs, would not be lured away by friends or visitors of the family. They might well, however, hear from friends, sisters or brothers who were in service elsewhere that there were advantageous vacancies at another house, and be able to act on those opportunities.

For the lady of the house the replacing of servants was a significant part of her life. She would, in the course of an average year, probably have three or four visits from the housekeeper to announce that: 'Please, Mum, the under-housemaid (or the scullery maid, or the second chambermaid) begs to give notice,' and have to go through the process of looking over candidates to replace them. To the exasperation of employers – and the situation is the same today in many places of work – these would no sooner have picked up the skills necessary to do their work efficiently, and to become familiar with the house routines, than they would be off to some other position.

It would be entirely usual for an experienced servant to have worked in five or six houses in the course of a twenty-year career. They would bring valuable experience with them to each new post, for despite the small differences in running each household that were dictated by family tradition or peccadilloes, the basic system would be similar, as would the servants' tasks and those who carried them out. It was relatively easy to move around from one job to another, and someone – such as a housekeeper – who was going on elsewhere might insist on bringing with her some of her erstwhile colleagues because they worked well as a team.

It was in the big houses that servants were more plentiful, more efficient, more rewarded, more likely to remain. It was here, too, that they stayed a part of the household long after they had vanished from the homes of middle-class people. In many suburban homes a maid, though useful, was a luxury, and to dispense with her, though it might cause inconvenience, would not reduce a house to chaos. In larger establishments servants were, of course, absolutely vital to the functioning of the household as well as to whatever work and leisure pursuits were undertaken by the family. Given the size of their homes, the simple process of keeping the building clean was likely to require a platoon of maids. Those families who had their own coach – it was a rarity to be 'carriage folk', and only in the latter part of the twentieth century would most people be able to afford a car – needed a coachman, grooms and stable boys to maintain the vehicle and the horses. Then there was the cooking of their meals and the serving of drinks and the conserving of game and the loading of guns. The receiving of visitors required specialist staff – footmen – and the dressing of both male and female employers in the complicated and elaborate clothing of the time made necessary another type of specialist: the valet and the lady's maid. It simply would not have been possible for a Victorian or Edwardian lady of the upper class to manage the putting up of her own hair or the putting on of many of the garments (think of the crinoline!) that fashion demanded she wear.

In other words, at the top of the household staff there were dedicated and experienced professionals, whose skills and knowledge were honed to a peak of excellence by years of training. Like any other professionals they would follow a career path, trading up from one household and one position to a better one. Wealthy people of the time could not have imagined doing without such servants, or even the less experienced general ones, in precisely the way that their present-day descendants could not be without electronic gadgets. Both groups would be lost without the things that they took for granted.

Inter-class relations were surprisingly good through-out British history. There was never the same level of smouldering animosity that sometimes emerged in coun-tries with a more authoritarian tradition or a more remote aristocracy – the classic example being that of France before the Revolution. Not since the Middle Ages had there been peasants, let alone serfs, in Britain. The gentry – the class below the aristocracy – was characterized in England by their ability to work informally with their tenants, and in Scotland, where Calvinism was a major social leveller and where the landowning class – proprietors of often unproductive estates – were not necessarily wealthy, the barriers between classes might well be even more blurred.

No doubt there were numerous idle, inefficient or incompetent servants, but the impression given by *Punch* is an exaggerated one. Most were good – or at the least adequate – at their jobs (they had after all been trained for them from childhood), inured to boredom and early rising, and with a physical stamina exhibited in endurance rather than outright strength. Routine can be a great comfort and, provided they kept to the rules laid down by their employer, they often had a level of security that contrasted favourably with that of people of the same class outside the estate walls.

Almost all households had sets of rules for servants. These were not just the large-lettered mottoes (WASTE NOT, WANT NOT!) that can still be seen painted on the walls of kitchens and servants' halls in great houses, but a detailed list of things that servants must or must not do. Some would be standard practice throughout society, and probably a matter of common sense. Others would be specific to the house. All would have to be learned quickly. These included the notion of always 'giving room' – standing aside, perhaps turning your back, but certainly not making eye contact, or verbal contact, with any of the upstairs inhabitants if one appeared in a corridor or on a staircase. A servant must also never sing or whistle while about their work, or indeed make any sort of noise that would draw attention to them. They could not call out to other servants in adjoining rooms. Must not talk to family or visitors unless asked a question, and must walk several paces behind upstairs inhabitants if carrying luggage for them. Very importantly, it was absolutely forbidden for a maid to hand anything to a member of the household without first putting it on a salver. Though largely taken for granted at the time, this custom sometimes caused trouble.

Margaret Powell was a very young and inexperienced maid when she was reprimanded for offering something straight to her employer. 'I thought it was terrible,' she later recalled, 'that someone could think you were so low that you couldn't even hand them anything out of your hands without it first being placed on a silver salver.' The point was surely less that servants were considered 'low' than that, given the dirtiness of much of the cleaning work in which they were engaged, they would be likely to pass on dust or oil from their hands.

Apart from this, there were rules regarding punctuality, especially at mealtimes since these were communal affairs. There were rules about drinking (despite the fact that servants were issued with beer) and about smoking (female servants were forbidden – or at the least expected not to do so). To be fair, some of the people upstairs – the family and guests – might well be subject to very similar rules. In numerous houses there have always been such lists, sometimes dealing with the same issues of drinking or smoking, and laying down rules that were often surprisingly severe. Etiquette books, which the British have always published and read in scores, go into considerable detail about the way to behave while a guest at a country house, including the advice that you ought to go for walks so as to give the hosts a rest from your company. As has already been seen, even those on the right side of the green baize door had to follow a code of conduct that could be very strict.

Like all servants, those employed in a great household were required to be as invisible as they could be when performing their duties. In eighteenth-century town houses it had been remarked upon that visitors might find the front door opened to them by a maid with a full chamber pot in her hand. This would not have happened in any well-run household, of course, and it was virtually impossible in the country houses of the Victorians. An intricate system of stairs and corridors meant that food and fuel could be carried between floors, servants could go to and from their duties, with broom or breakfast tray, without the family or their guests having to see them. Should a servant meet on a main staircase a member of the household, they were usually required to turn their backs, and would certainly not speak. These customs may seem over-formal and unnecessary to modern sensibilities, but like most forms of etiquette they represented a structure that actually made life simpler and less awkward than it would otherwise have been.

The nineteenth-century author Robert Kerr wrote: 'The family constitute one community: the servants another. Whatever may be to their mutual regard and confidence as dwellers under the same roof, each class is entitled to shut its door upon the other. On both sides this privacy is highly valued.' Under normal conditions the owner's family would not venture into the servants' territory without an invitation.

The eccentric Duke of Portland would have dismissed any housemaid who met him in the corridors of his house, Welbeck Abbey. He was not alone in this. One maid who was fascinated enough to stare at her employer as he sat in his dressing gown in an adjoining room did not realize she had been observed. Later that day, when the servants were assembled, the butler announced that whichever young woman had been spying on the master was to take notice. It was certainly customary that the family would not greet any servant whom they met. To some masters servants were simply machines, going about their work to make the house run smoothly, and one would no more speak to them than to a clock or a carriage horse.

Yet masters varied as much as any other disparate group of people. There were also families who saw their servants as friends, or at least regarded them with interest. Naturally the length of time they had been in employment and the extent to which they were part of the life of the house could make a difference to the way they were treated. If servants proved over time their loyalty and discretion, they could reasonably expect some favour at the end of their working lives, such as residence in a local alms house or a cottage tucked away on the estate. They might alternatively be set up in a pub. The number of hostelries that have taken the names of aristocrats and have names like the Duke of Sutherland or the Marquess of Zetland reflects the kindness of employers who enabled their former butlers or house-keepers to retire into this occupation. The tradition went back at least to the eighteenth century, for the Marquess of Granby, heir to the Dukedom of Rutland and an officer in the Army, made a practice of establishing his men, once discharged from service, as landlords of public houses. So many of them expressed their gratitude that the Marquess of Granby is still a very common name for English pubs to this day.

Though there was no old-age pension, servants had no outlay to make on food or accommodation, and therefore it was often possible for them to save a large percentage of their wages. Those who did not have to send remittances to relatives could accumulate, over the years, a sum in the hundreds or even the thousands. They might also benefit from a master's will, for it was surprisingly common that employers left individual sums to their servants, a stipulated amount to be settled on each.

Another form of kindness which they might experience was the servants' dance, an annual entertainment at which they were waited upon by other servants who had been hired in for the evening. There would also be an orchestra to entertain the guests. If the household were especially liberal, the maids might even be allowed to invite followers, provided they were sufficiently respectable (in other words, regular and known).

Some employers were exceptionally good to their staff. The Duchess of Richmond not only held a party for her servants every Christmas, but also took her maids to the theatre in London and to tea at the Grosvenor Hotel. There were other mistresses who arranged similar outings, enabling the maids to experience the world of upstairs, for a few hours at least.

Rather than receiving help as a gift, some servants were able to earn their way to a better future. Many ex-domestics were able to save enough to open a small shop, restaurant, pub or seaside boarding house. (Mrs and Mrs Hudson, in the series *Upstairs, Downstairs*, do the latter when their employer's house is sold.) Senior servants – butlers and housekeepers – made enough in tips and presents to retire very comfortably.

In a happy household the servants would not wish to

move on, particularly the senior ones, and there would be little scope for advancement among those lower down the hierarchy. Employers were known to be unhappy and irritated when servants gave their notice. Though they had the power to remove a servant from their household at very short notice, they did not like servants, as it were, to remove themselves. They did not like the thought of having to search for replacements, or the possibility that no one would be found who was suitable. They did not like the thought of a new servant making mistakes and trying the patience of the household while learning the job. The only time they showed pleasure at the departure of a servant was if that person was getting married. Those who stayed and worked in a family throughout their career would find it increasingly difficult as they grew older. Men and women over fifty had little prospect of finding other work, because they were seen as too old for the heavy lifting and carrying that was involved. For a very large number of old servants with ungenerous employers the only prospect they faced was the workhouse.

The number of servants employed in a house varied, understandably, according to what was going on there. At different times of the year there would be less need for a full staff, while during a time of frequent entertainments, such as at Christmas or during the hunting and shooting seasons, it might well be necessary to hire in additional servants. There were usually sources of supplementary manpower available locally. If necessary, outdoor staff could be brought in to help serve at meals, or waiters lured from a restaurant in some nearby town (though these were considered to lack the necessary finesse). Maids and footmen could also summon brothers and sisters.

The yearly routine varied from family to family. Those who lived in very grand houses and belonged to the high aristocracy would probably have several country houses as well as a residence in London. They would visit these other properties either for a change of scene or for reasons of duty or pleasure. For instance if the head of the family held a position at Court, he and his wife might be required to spend weeks or months in London or at Windsor. If the family were keen sportsmen they would want to spend the autumn on grouse moors in Scotland or Yorkshire. During the summer they would in all probability be attending the events of the London Season. Wherever it was they were going, they would take with them the servants they needed and leave the rest behind on 'boarding' or board wages. In other words, wages that were somewhat more generous than usual to compensate for the fact that the servants, in the absence of the family, were not able to receive their usual benefits of upstairs leftovers. The valet and lady's maid would without question have gone, the butler might have, but the housekeeper would not. The servants who remained in the country would have much less to do without the need for daily clearing up and serving meals.

When families went to London for the Season, they might well have a town residence with a skeleton staff retained there. Just before Easter servants from the country house would go up to town to help clean the house. The Season began in May and might involve up to ten balls a night. Racing took place at Epsom and Ascot. There were the usual other sporting events, including the Eton and Harrow cricket match and the regattas at Cowes and Henley. The Royal Academy Summer Exhibition was also important. Two additions in the twentieth century made the Season more varied: the Chelsea Flower Show and the opera at Glyndebourne. The servants, though likely to be as busy as their masters, had time to see something of London, to visit music halls and shops or to go dancing. The Season of course revolved around the presentations at Court, though these were important only for those with daughters 'coming out' that year. Events came to a close in August when the grouse moors beckoned and the aristocracy decamped to Scotland or the north of England to spend the autumn in country pursuits.

Those whose role it was to care for the country house stayed in it. The house and its plate and wine cellars still needed protecting. The remaining servants still needed supervising, and numerous tasks in the kitchen, the stables and the estate needed to continue. The gardens could not be neglected. The most important task was the thorough annual cleaning of the house, from basement to rafters, which could last four to five weeks and which must be completed in time for the owner's return. The chairs and sofas would be hidden under dust sheets to protect them. All repainting or wallpapering would have been saved for this interlude. The estate carpenter would be kept busy mending furniture. Despite all this activity, the summer would have been a relatively carefree time for the servants. They could enjoy a feeling of relaxation, wandering at will through the upstairs rooms, sitting in the gardens in their free time, larking about in the servants' hall in the knowledge that they could make as much noise as they wanted. Once the bulk of the work had been accomplished, many of the servants could also perhaps take a short holiday and travel home to see their families. Those who hailed from poor rural communities could expect to enjoy considerable status when they returned, looking clean and prosperous in non-uniform clothes that were hardly ever worn, bringing with them money to spend or to give away, as well as produce from the estate such as hams or preserves, and stories of their employers and colleagues that would entertain the neighbours.

Once the family returned from London or a sporting destination, autumn merged into winter and there was little to do on the land. This was the season for hunting and shooting. No other activities have come to be so closely identified with the English gentleman. The fox-hunt was, and is, a tribal affair, for there are different hunts in different parts of the country and each is under the care of a Master of Foxhounds. Though sportsmen would become members of a particular hunt, they could easily travel (thanks to the railway, which provided horseboxes) to other areas and hunt as guests. Enthusiasts naturally did this, keen to experience different country and different packs. The hunting season lasted, as did the shooting of game birds, from August until Easter.

House parties lasted from Friday until Tuesday, when the visitors' book was signed and servants were given a tip (known as a 'vail').

By the late nineteenth century servants had one half-day off a month – Sunday, so that they could attend church. They might also get a day every month. They would have little choice as to when this could be taken, for they had to suit not their own convenience but that of their employer. Servants in a town would sometimes ask for leave to go to church so that they could get away from the house for a few hours, and go to visit friends. Their employer would not normally question them about their whereabouts, unless they had been gone longer than expected. In the country there was usually little choice as to place of worship, and the servants would attend the parish church, probably going there in a body and sitting (of course) separately in the gallery or the back pews. They would have worn their best, non-uniform clothes, though these would not be eye-catching. The guidelines they received on taking up employment would have made it clear that off-duty dress must be plain in style and sober in colour.

Attendance at church did not mean that servants had the rest of the day off, for there were many household tasks that still had to be performed. The chambermaids would have to tidy bedrooms as on every other day; the valets and lady's maids would be working as hard as ever to dress the family for church; the meals on a Sunday often being the most elaborate of the week, the kitchens would be busy throughout the day. Not all servants could be spared for religious observance, and they were likely to have had to go in shifts. In the Victorian and Edwardian eras there were, in any case, three services a day in many churches. Apart from matins and evensong there was an afternoon service, and that would have coincided with the rest period of those who had spent the morning cooking or peeling vegetables.

Religion was seen as important to the running of a good household. It encouraged the status quo. Christianity brought with it a moral code that was useful for encouraging servants to behave themselves and to accept their place in the world. Most employers thought it important to set an example by at least going through the motions of observance.

The bigger the household the more specialist servants there would be, and the more exotic their functions. There could be a wine butler who only looked after the cellar and served at meals, just as there is a specialist wine waiter in restaurants today. He would not have been required, or willing, to supervise the footmen or answer the door. There would very likely be a chef just for pastries and desserts – again, something that is still common in restaurants. There could in addition be kitchen servants who would only deal with preparing vegetables. King Edward VII, both after his accession and when he was Prince of Wales, took with him on visits to country houses his own catering staff, which included a boy whose only task was to make coffee for him.

As well as a valet, the master of the house might have a groom of the chamber, a title that today only exists in royal households and which in practice meant a young man who generally tidied the bedroom and ran baths. Such servants were, one presumes, the very antithesis of the rushed-off-her-feet, overworked housemaid. While some servants clearly had more work to do than they could get through in the course of a day, others suffered from the opposite extreme. Those with little to do spent hours of every day standing about waiting to be

summoned and employed. Boredom was a common
enemy, and a cause of many men leaving their positions,
and indeed service. This was especially true of footmen,
who came into their own during the afternoons when
social calls were made and received. From luncheon
onwards they would have been positioned in the front
hall of the house to listen for the sounds of approaching
vehicles, so as to be ready to open the doors and take
coats and accept visiting cards on salvers. Alternatively,
of course, they would have outdoor capes and hats in
readiness to accompany their mistress on visits of her
own, both of them standing up behind her carriage.
When she arrived at her destination they would both
dismount and walk in unison to the front door, one to
knock and the other to enquire if the mistress of the
house was at home.

The butler, or the steward if there was one, was
unquestionably the head of the servant body. Traditionally, a big household was run by a steward, the usual title
on the Continent for this functionary, and a title so
ancient that it is mentioned in the Bible (Pharaoh's
steward is one of those whose dream is interpreted by
Joseph). Though far more women than men worked in
domestic service, the highest-ranking servant was always
a male – the steward and/or butler automatically took
precedence over the housekeeper even though she
probably knew the house better than he did. Men were
generally paid more, and were far less disadvantaged. In
a very large household, there could be a steward in
overall charge with a butler, ranking beneath him,
responsible for the wine cellar and the supervision of

footmen. If there were no steward, the butler would by default become responsible for the administration of the household. If there were no valet he would have to provide that service for his master too. If there were no footmen he would have to answer the door, announce guests and fetch their coats when they departed. At mealtimes he was present in the dining room. He might be the only server at luncheon, while at supper he would have the assistance of footmen. He would place the first course on the table before summoning the family to dine, and would then stand behind his master's chair unless, of course, there were no footmen and once again he had to fill that role himself.

The butler wore a dark suit. In the evenings, when the family and their friends changed into tails he did so too. Though this made him look from a distance like someone from 'upstairs', the difference would have been obvious to anyone who knew the customs of this world. He wore a black bow tie in the evenings while the family and their friends wore white. He supervised the service at mealtimes, and poured the wine unless there was a wine butler to do so.

He did not have charge of the valets, who answered direct to the family member for whom they worked, but he was in charge of other indoor male servants. In an average-sized household, he was, first and foremost, responsible for the wine cellar and other drinks. He traditionally kept the key to the cellar, and thus according to popular perception was often drunk. Similarly he was charged with responsibility for the plate, which would be kept in a safe or a strong room. This would usually be sited next to his pantry and reachable only through the room in which he slept, so that he could protect it.

In John Galsworthy's short story about the Forsyte family, 'Revolt at Roger's', can be seen the paradoxical difficulty that these two responsibilities could create as Smith, the family butler, comes to grief: 'When the house of Roger Forsyte was burgled in the autumn of 1870, Smith was drunk and made no serious attempt to rebut the accusation. To be drunk without anyone knowing is a tort; to be discovered drunk, a misdemeanour; to be drunk when burglary is committed under one's nose, a crime. This, at least, was Roger's view, and he acted on it by immediate dismissal. His spoons had gone and Smith must go too.' The butler was also responsible for opening the door to visitors, and his domain, on the ground floor or in a basement, would often have a window commanding a view of the drive so that approaching vehicles could be seen and recognized in time for him to welcome their occupants and announce the visitors on their arrival.

No other figure among the servants was so familiar, so potent or so powerful as the butler. He is also one of the great stock characters of English fiction. The notion that the chief male servant in a household has a respectable status of his own – that he is a 'gentleman's gentleman', and displays qualities of wisdom, discretion, courage, stoicism or generosity – is a very English concept. Other servant figures in literature, both in Britain and elsewhere, have traditionally been characterized by craftiness, laziness, venality and an inclination to join in any mischief that is going on, such as helping a young lady to elope. They appear this way in Shakespeare, and – to take other well-known examples – in Mozart's operas and Molière's plays. They are comic creations, and their appearance is normally the cue for some buffoonery or other. They are a world removed from the figure of Jeeves or of Bunter, the manservant of Lord Peter Wimsey in Dorothy L. Sayers' detective novels. These men too appear for the purpose of amusing the reader, but it is their droll acceptance of the absurdity of their employers that provides the humour, or the manner in which they rescue them from the scrapes that their impulsiveness gets them into. They themselves command the respect of the reader.

Stevens, the butler in Kazuo Ishiguro's novel *The Remains of the Day*, muses on why this is so:

> Butlers only truly exist in England. Other countries, whatever title is actually used, have only manservants. Continentals are unable to be butlers because they are incapable of emotional restraint, which only the English race is capable of. [They] cannot control themselves in moments of strong emotion, and are thus unable to maintain a professional demeanour. For this reason when you think of a great butler he is bound, almost by definition, to be an Englishman.

There is no question that this stoical, unflappable nature was and is the quality most admired in the successful butler. He was required to be present at all manner of important, or awkward, or embarrassing moments in the family's life, and he must not visibly react. He must be discreet and not gossip about what he had seen or heard. He must be able to deal with any number of unexpected situations – fire and flood, attempted burglary, quarrels among the other servants, deaths or illnesses, affairs between guests or family members. He often owed his position to the trust he had earned from the family, and a good butler was greatly valued. Because he had reached the top of his profession, he was not usually looking for further career opportunities, and was more likely to remain with his employers until retirement.

Lady Cynthia Asquith, who came from a servant-owning background, remarked that one thing even good butlers could not always control was their reaction to the conversation of the dinner guests. She said: 'Few butlers, however imposing their mien and deportment, were above being visibly, at times audibly, amused by dining-room jokes or mishaps.'

The cartoonist H. M. Bateman, one of England's greatest lampooners of the twentieth-century middle class, produced a drawing called 'The maid who was but human'. The young woman is serving potatoes while one of the guests tells an amusing story. The others laugh, but when the maid also bursts out laughing, the guests all look up in horror and then carry on with their meal in embarrassed silence. A perfect butler, or any other servant, would not be guilty of such a gaffe, no matter what the temptation, but who could blame them if this was not always possible?

While Wodehouse's Lord Emsworth has all the characteristics of the dotty aristocrat that readers enjoy and expect, P. G. Wodehouse's most famous creation, Jeeves, shares the sense of unflappability seen in the butlers of numerous country-house murder novels – an ability to remain calm when all around them guests and family members are being found dead in suspicious circumstances. Most people have never met a real butler, and it is possible that Wodehouse himself was not familiar with the breed, but he wrote of them in a manner already established by the likes of Oscar Wilde and J. M. Barrie, and the stereotype of a butler thus created is one that the British, and the rest of the world, have taken to their hearts. It is surely an image on which real members of this honourable profession still model themselves.

Yet the fictional manservants of Wodehouse and Barrie and Agatha Christie occasionally had their counterparts in reality. Roger Childs was butler, for two decades or so from just after the First World War, to John Christie (no relation of the authoress). Christie, scion of a large landowning family, was the owner of Glyndebourne in Sussex, in the grounds of which he built the famous opera house. Childs entered Christie's employ as a manservant when the latter was a bachelor master teaching mathematics at Eton, and remained with him until his death in 1940. The distinction between a valet and a butler was sometimes minimal, and Childs would have graduated to the latter, more senior, post when his master moved to a larger house.

Childs was the epitome of the unflappable butler. When John Christie was to read a lesson in the parish church one Sunday and could not find the place, Childs – who was in a pew nearby – prompted him in a stage whisper from the congregation, but said afterwards: 'I think, sir, it would be better if *I* read the lessons in future.' And so he did. He regarded his employer's marriage in 1931 as a 'lapse', yet remained in his service. In fact, Christie asked him to be best man at the wedding and to stand godfather to his eldest son. Childs' employer was a man of marked eccentricities, and gestures of this sort therefore did not seem out of place in him. It would have been unthinkable, however, for most families' butlers to be given such privileges. In his spare time Childs ran a local scout troop (which collected the money at early Glyndebourne recitals) and, delightfully, took part in one of the operas in a non-singing minor role. During the 1935 season he was paid fifteen guineas – the going rate for an *artiste* – to appear as the 'Dumb Servant' in the production of *The Abduction from the Seraglio*, and brought the house down with a hilarious performance. One suspects that, had he been required to take one of the leads and sing an aria, he would have done so with similar aplomb. Clearly able to turn his hand to anything, he was greatly missed by Christie when he died. His employer had him buried beneath a handsome stone, inscribed in Latin, in the nearby church at Ringmer.

The butler continues to be a major character in fiction and in films. Arguably the most famous English screen butler of all is one who is virtually unknown in Britain itself or in the United States. 'James' is one of only two characters in an eighteen-minute comedy film called *Dinner for One*, made in 1963. This short piece is perennially popular in Scandinavia and throughout the German-speaking countries. In Germany itself it is watched by up to half the population every New Year's Eve – indeed it is as much a part of the celebrations as singing 'Auld Lang Syne' would be in Britain. The story deals with an elderly lady who annually dines with her oldest friends. All of them have long-since died, but she maintains the fiction that they are present at her table, and toasts are poured for them to drink. Her butler (magnificently played by the comedian Freddie Frinton) pretends to be each of them in turn, filling – and emptying – their glasses. He becomes more and more inebriate, but manages to serve impeccably.

The notion of the butler as a man who can do anything is seen to even greater effect in J. M. Barrie's play *The Admirable Crichton*, which was first staged in 1902 – at the height of the Edwardian 'golden age'. Its central character is the usual model of rectitude – a butler who knows his place and ensures that the other servants keep to theirs. When his master Lord Loam institutes the well-meant practice of inviting the entire servants' hall to tea once a month, during which they are waited on by the family, the occasion is hated in equal measure by the servants and their betters – not least by Crichton who is shown to be the wisest character in the play.

In the film version there is an exchange about this that is revealing. Encouraged by the loosening of hierarchical bonds within the household, the page boy, on hearing that the servants are to be invited upstairs, says: 'I reckon it'll be all friends together, eh, Crichton?' He is told by the butler, who is played by Kenneth More: 'You might, one day if you work hard, reach a position in which you may call me *"Mister* Crichton".' In fact, the boy is at once dismissed from his post, for having taken the liberty of addressing the head of the servants' hall with such familiarity. This would have happened in any genuine Edwardian household, as well as in any office or other place of work.

Both play and film go on to show that, when the

family is shipwrecked while cruising on their yacht, it is the butler's initiative, and not the 'natural leadership' of the aristocracy, that saves the situation. Yet when at the end they are rescued from the island after two years, masters and servants all resume their former places as if nothing has happened, despite having lived on equal terms and learned a great deal about each other in the meantime. A character they encounter once back at home, the formidable Lady Brocklehurst, quizzes the servants to ensure that the proprieties were upheld. She is reassured on being told that throughout their exile the domestics took their meals separately from the family. The play is very funny, but it makes the point that there must be such a hierarchy if an ordered way of life is to be maintained.

It is sometimes remarked that employers and their servants lived only feet apart but had little to do with each other. This is true, but perhaps not so unnatural or out of the ordinary as we might imagine. How many people today live only feet from their next-door neighbours yet know nothing about them? Servants inhabited a parallel universe. Their lives were governed by a mysterious timetable of which most family members remained in ignorance, carrying out tasks that were largely unseen and overlooked. Their names, if they were maids or footmen, might well not even be the ones they'd been christened with. The accepted convention among both employers and servants was that each side should leave the other alone. Servants were there to be busy, and any talking to them would only be wasting their time and getting them into trouble. Besides, the inhabitants upstairs did not want any further intimacy with those who already knew so much about them, while the servants' own lives remained mysterious to their employers. It would make for a very unequal relationship.

Not every butler was trained to the life of a servant, and it would be wrong to assume that it was necessary to have spent a lifetime learning the duties and preparing for the role. Though the responsibilities could be considerable, the tasks were not especially complicated, and a matter of days or weeks would be enough to familiarize a man with what was required of him. Anyone with the appropriate manner – a certain natural presence, an authoritative voice, an undemonstrative nature and the ability to remain calm in the midst of domestic crises – could make an effective butler. In the first series of *Downton Abbey*, one of the most delightful moments is provided when it is revealed that Carson, who surely was intended by nature to be a manservant in a great household, has at an earlier stage in life been one of a pair of stage comedians in the music halls, called 'The Cheerful Charlies'. In fact a stage career, though certainly not seen as respectable, would have been invaluable training, for it would have required similar qualities of confidence, timing and voice projection. Such is Carson's imperturbability that he is able to survive this public exposure with his dignity intact – a sure sign that he is made of the right stuff!

A butler was less likely to find his way into the affections of family members than other servants, such as the nurserymaid or the cook (doubtless generations of children learned to obtain food between meals by wheedling from the latter). Sometimes, however, he could become a pronounced influence on members of his master's household. Henry Moat was butler at Renishaw, ancestral home of the Sitwell family. The children who grew up there in the last years of the Victorian era – Edith, Osbert and Sacheverell Sitwell – all went on to become influential figures in the arts. The children had a distant relationship with their parents, but Osbert found an ally and a mentor in Moat. A man of intelligence and wide reading, he possessed a general knowledge that enabled him to answer many of the boy's questions and to channel his curiosity in profitable directions. When in later life Osbert appeared in *Who's Who*, he described his education as having been obtained 'during holidays from Eton'. Moat, who was by that time living in retirement, took this statement as a compliment, writing to his charge that:

> I see in Monday's *Scarborough News* a bit ... saying your education was not got at school or college but during your holidays. Well, sir, I make bold to claim some of that, because if you wanted to know anything about things on the earth, the sea, under the earth or in the air above you generally came to me, even when you had a tutor, and often the tutors came too.

The butler's female counterpart was the housekeeper. Like him, she had reached the top of the tree in domestic service. She was one of the 'Pugs' or senior servants. She ran the still room, in which preserves were made and bottled, as well as keeping the linen cupboard and the china cabinets in order. She was not required to wear uniform, and her everyday dress was a badge of rank, as was the immense bunch of keys that she inevitably carried. She supervised the maids, inspecting their dress each day, and liaised with the mistress to discuss the day's business each morning. If her employers went on a journey, it was her responsibility to welcome them back by standing at the front door or at the top of the entrance steps. It was also her task to greet visitors and show them to their rooms. She was responsible for ordering provisions and for dealing with tradesmen, and these individuals would have thought it well worth the trouble of keeping on her good side, perhaps with bribes or presents, to ensure that business continued to come their way. To those under her authority, and sometimes even to members of the upstairs family, she could be terrifying.

Besides her commission from local tradesmen, she often received tips from guests, and had the right to sell off-cuts of meat and other edible odds and ends from the kitchen. She might also smuggle food out of the house to send home to her family. Hers was a lucrative post, and sometimes astonishingly so if the house were sufficiently historic or interesting. There was good money to be made from showing visitors around. Mrs Hume, housekeeper at Warwick Castle in the early years of the nineteenth century, left at her death a fortune in tips and wages totalling many thousands of pounds. Enough in fact to have built a country house of her own!

In very grand houses the cook might be a man, for a foreign chef was a prestigious thing to have, but mostly this task was carried out by women. The cook was next in importance to the housekeeper, for she had the only slightly less onerous responsibility of feeding a community that might well number hundreds of people. The kitchen was often at some distance from the dining room – a deliberate ploy to prevent the smells of cooking, and perhaps the noise, from reaching the polite part of the house. If female she was always addressed as 'Mrs', whether or not she was married, as a sign of respect. There were two types of cook, differentiated by title: a plain cook and a trained cook. The former dealt with feeding the other servants on basic fare. The latter was able to cope with multiple courses and more exotic fare for the employer and his family. Because the feeding of a community so large, both upstairs and downstairs, was a major undertaking, the authority of the cook was correspondingly great. She had absolute authority over the kitchen maids, and no one would fail to show her appropriate respect, or enter her territory without permission. A sign in the Victorian kitchens at Rockingham Castle in Northamptonshire makes clear that this is the cook's domain: 'No person Whether belonging to the Family or Not is ever under any pretcxt to enter the Kitchen without obtaining leave. RING the BELL.'

The youngest members of the culinary staff were the kitchen and scullery maids, who would start work there at fourteen years old or even younger. The scullery maids were the ones who did the washing of dishes and the peeling of vegetables, while the kitchen maids helped the cook by preparing the less important parts of a dish. The cook could be as great a tyrant as the housekeeper. She would supervise not only the cooking but the washing of pots and dishes and the cleaning of ovens, stoves, floors and surfaces; even with the lesser knowledge of food hygiene that there was at the time, these kitchen areas had to be kept spotless. Mice were a constant nuisance and, apart from setting traps, were got rid of by organizing periodic hunts using the gardeners' dogs.

Eating was something that went on all day in a wealthy Victorian or Edwardian household. The notion of eating sparingly, or even sensibly, did not seriously occur to the middle and upper classes. They would overindulge and then take periodic curative treatment, perhaps once a year at a foreign spa. Cereal and toast would not have been regarded as a nearly adequate start to the day, and cereal was, in any case, only for invalids. Instead they ate very large breakfasts of numerous dishes – kedgeree, bacon and eggs, and game. There would then be mid-morning snacks prepared for them, such as boiled eggs and toast. Luncheon, a much heavier repast than we would expect today, would follow within two hours or so, and afternoon tea would be a substantial meal in itself, with sandwiches and cake and jams that the cook would have made. Dinner would be of four or five courses, and later in the evening there would be more sandwiches laid out for anyone who was feeling peckish. All of this food not only shortened the life expectancy of those who ate it but considerably lengthened the day of those who prepared it. The kitchen would be kept working throughout every waking hour to keep up with the demands made on it, and the dishes produced were not only numerous but very complicated. The cook might well be preparing half a dozen sauces at once.

As shown, the vast majority of children who went into service came from backgrounds of extreme poverty.

Their parents had numerous other offspring, and needed them out of the house and earning a wage as soon as possible. Becoming a servant was considered a respectable, and even prestigious, move. And for a few of these impoverished children it turned out to be the passport to a life they could never have imagined living.

Rosa Ovenden (1867–1952), who would become known by her married surname of Lewis, had a background typical of girls who went into service. The daughter of an undertaker, she was born at Leyton in Essex and left school at the age of twelve to become a maid-of-all-work. After four years she happened to be employed by exiled royalty, for she joined the domestic staff of the French Pretender, Philippe, Count of Paris. Here she was able to learn French cookery – allegedly from the great chef Escoffier himself – at a time when the Paris-led culinary fashion was changing towards a lighter cuisine than the heavy fare on which the mid-Victorians had lived. She was therefore in a household that was not only in the forefront of culinary innovation but at the very top of Society. Clearly hard-working and intelligent, she quickly developed her cookery skills and became Head Kitchen Maid. Maids did not normally do the cooking, but Rosa possessed enough ability, and confidence, to be allowed to do so even for very important visitors. The most sought-after of all Victorian dinner guests – the Prince of Wales – was so impressed with the results that he asked to meet her. They were to become friends (and possibly lovers) and he would keep a benevolent eye on her career.

She moved to the home of another French émigré, the Duke of Orleans, but also branched out into what would now be called 'freelance' work, travelling to the homes of the wealthy to provide splendid dinners for their guests. Among her first clients was Lady Randolph Churchill, daughter-in-law of the Duke of Marlborough, mother of Winston, and – through her beauty and wit – one of the leaders of Society. Rosa Lewis's reputation was made, and for a time – until the outbreak of war put paid to lavish entertaining – she was responsible for a large proportion of the private dinners given by London's *beau monde*. In 1902 she was able, without interrupting her culinary career, to buy the Cavendish Hotel in London's Jermyn Street. She would remain its *chatelaine* until her death, indomitably surviving both wartime bombing and at least one stroke.

Rosa hobnobbed with aristocracy, counted royalty among her admirers (she was sent a signed photograph by the Kaiser, which she contemptuously hung in the lavatory when war broke out in 1914), and lived on a social plane that would have been unthinkable for those with whom she had started in service. She did this, moreover, without any attempt at remaking herself in the image of the upper class. Though she dressed well and could look like a lady, she made no effort to speak, or to behave, like one. She was brash, noisy and outspoken enough to strike fear in a duke or a general, but showed frequent kindness both to employees and to impecunious guests. She is an object lesson for anyone believing English Society to be a tight-knit club from which incomers will always be excluded by virtue of their accent, or lack of wealth, or gender. Rosa Lewis proved that powerful friends, originality, personality and outstanding ability can help anyone bridge the gap between a lowly birth and a celebrated life.

She even found a place in English literature when she was used as the model for the character Lottie Crump in Evelyn Waugh's novel *Vile Bodies*. Given the appellation 'the queen of cooks', she was also known as the Duchess of Jermyn Street. In the 1970s, a quarter-century after she died, her life became the subject of a BBC drama series, though given a thin coating of fiction (the central character, Louisa Trotter, becomes proprietress of the Bentinck Hotel and is dubbed eponymously *The Duchess of Duke Street*).

Though actresses and singers could and did become the toast of fashionable London, and though marrying chorus girls was not unheard of among aristocratic sons (who were known as 'stage-door Johnnies'), Rosa Lewis was the only former domestic to scale the social heights through doing what servants do. She represented, of course, a case so rare as to be unique, and perhaps any other woman would have lacked her novelty value. Nevertheless she proved what could be accomplished, given luck and talent and perseverance.

There were other members of a household staff who were neither one thing nor the other. They did not take their meals with the family, but neither would they have considered dining in the servants' hall. They were as educated – and quite possibly more so – than their employers, and might have pretensions to gentility themselves. Grand country houses would, if the owners had sufficient spirituality or concern for respectability, employ a chaplain. There would also be a librarian, who perhaps acted as curator of other collections too (given the quantities of stuffed birds and butterflies, fossils and minerals, prints and etchings, that many upper-class households accumulated). There might also be a tutor to teach the sons of the household until they went away to school. He was responsible not only for giving them sufficient command of Classical languages for admission to a public school but might even, in isolated cases, teach them how to box. It was usually this hapless individual whose task it was to tell his charges the facts of life when they reached a suitable age. If the family was sufficiently sporting, there might even be a cricket professional or a swimming instructor, though these would not be resident servants and would appear only when their skills were required.

It might well have been the case that three positions were filled by the same man. A chaplain would have nothing much to do on weekdays, and looking after the library and collections would be a suitably dignified pastime for him. He was by definition a man of respectability and learning – he would be a university graduate – and therefore qualified to teach young people. To be chaplain in such a household would be a useful start to a young man's clerical career, for if he gave satisfaction he might perhaps be granted a lucrative living that was in the gift of his employer.

For the daughters of the house, for whom going away to school was not a custom or even a possibility until the end of the nineteenth century, there would be a governess. This latter figure is among the most poignant members of the country-house population. Usually a gentlewoman of straitened means – and sometimes a poor relation of the family – she lacked the means or connections to marry and was obliged to devote her life to educating more fortunate girls whose background was often similar to her own. She was not treated as part of the family but as an employee who could be got rid of when her work was done. She was not accepted by the servants because she was from a class above their own. Governesses often existed in a sad limbo between upstairs and downstairs, and were in many cases foreigners and thus doubly suspect. They might be French or German or perhaps Swiss, for part of their function was to teach one or more languages to their charges. Generations of girls grew up in the shadow of these spinsters, caricatured – or remembered – as strict and humourless and exacting, who supervised their lessons and piano practice, and marched them round the park in all weathers for their daily walk.

The lady's maid ranked below the housekeeper and the cook in the hierarchy of female servants. She was probably by background a more respectable, well-spoken servant – perhaps lower-middle-class in origin – than those who were recruited for the kitchen, and she was the equivalent of the gentleman's valet. This meant that she waited upon the mistress of the house, or some other lady member of the family, but worked for no one else. She brought tea in the mornings and drew back the curtains, ran baths, collected cast-off clothing and took it to be washed or mended. She dressed her mistress's hair – an operation that could take up a considerable amount of her time – and dressed her for all the events that would fill her day, providing day dresses, outdoor clothes, tennis dresses, dinner dresses, ballgowns, on cue. At night she would warm her employer's nightgown and lay it out on the bed. Storing, selecting, preparing and fitting all of these garments was a considerable responsibility, given the number of times in a day that a lady would change clothes under the strict rules of Victorian etiquette.

The lady's maid wore a black or grey dress to look appropriately sober. She may have been qualified to assist and advise her mistress on her wardrobe – and indeed was expected to be aware of new styles and fashions – but she was not allowed to display any sartorial flair of her own.

The lady's maid travelled with her employer and thus had the chance to visit other country houses, and to go abroad. She would probably have the ability to sew, so as to carry out urgent repairs and run up basic garments. Those who aspired to be lady's maids would often train in dressmaking and millinery for a few years before they entered service. In a small household they might then go straight into a position with a lady. In a larger house they could well be employed as an assistant to the existing lady's maid, or be put into service with one of the daughters of the house as a sort of probation. Foreign maids were sometimes in fashion, though they must be able to speak fluent English and to adjust to life in Britain. Those of French origin were expected to be well up on fashion, though the Swiss were also popular as both male and female servants.

A lady's maid was ultimately responsible for every aspect of the appearance of her mistress, with all the complex and intricate tasks that this required. These even included expertise in cosmetics, for she must keep her mistress not only well dressed but as young-looking as possible. A good maid would have a host of useful tips and remedies with which to help her employer. She would have her own recipes for skin lotions and even for shoe polish, and would have an expert knowledge of how to mix the potions necessary to remove stains from clothing. Throughout the whole of this era her most important function, as Mrs Beeton declared, was her ability to act as hairdresser. Because no one woman – especially one in her twenties, as so many lady's maids were – could be expected to have a working knowledge of all the latest hairstyles, a lady's maid was often sent on courses to learn them. One thing she did not have to spend much time on, however, was washing hair, for Edwardian ladies did not believe in this. Thinking that the process would do damage by coarsening hair and leaving split ends, it was seen as preferable instead for it to be brushed regularly, and for long periods, by a maid using a clean brush. This was considered as effective a means of avoiding dandruff as any shampoo. The hair would of course also be scented.

Though qualified by her position to dine in the 'Pugs' Parlour' and have tea brought to her in the mornings by a more junior servant, the life of a lady's maid was not necessarily an easy one. She would have to accompany her mistress everywhere, keeping very long hours during social events. Throughout the Season, for instance, she would have to sit up until her lady returned from a ball in the early hours of the morning and be ready to undress her, brush her hair and put her to bed, before taking the cast-off clothing away to be cleaned or mended. Through the day and night, at all times of the year, she must be able to be at her mistress' side at once, and therefore usually slept in an adjoining bedroom. Like many servants, however, she might not see her own bed until all her tasks were completed, and she must accustom herself to getting by on very little sleep.

A lady's maid was always addressed as 'Miss', whether or not she was married – though in practice this would have been an extremely difficult life for any woman who was living with a husband and it is likely, given the comparative youth of many of these maids, that if they married at all, they put it off until they had left service.

The gentleman's valet had an equivalent knowledge of masculine dress, and would undoubtedly be capable of basic sewing. He could put on a shirt button or mend a tear, though he would certainly not run up entire garments the way a lady's maid would do. He would be able to brush and sponge clothes, press them, remove all manner of stains, pack and unpack for his master, strop a razor and shave him, clean his shoes and boots (though in most houses this was the job of a junior servant) and even select the flower for his buttonhole. He would often have his own recipes for shaving-soap and shoe polish, and might blend his own cologne. If he were really skilful he could perhaps cut his employer's hair as well. Since he accompanied his master on his travels he would need to be well versed in reading railway timetables, in booking tickets, in dealing with foreign customs and hotel staff, and in finding his way around the United Kingdom and other countries. It is from this that the notion of the ultra-capable, Jeeves-like servant derives. He could sometimes speak the main continental lan- guages and interpret for his master. Some valets, because they tended to be men of resourcefulness and ability, took courses in French or German to increase their usefulness and enhance their position. As well as this, a valet often acted as assistant for his master in various sporting capacities. He would frequently serve as loader during shoots, standing behind his master with the pair to his shotgun and waiting to reload the one just fired. He might even act as caddy during golf matches, or know how to re-string a tennis racket.

A paragon like this did not come cheap. He was well paid for the services he provided and he could make handsome tips as well. There was considerable scope to expand on his basic duties and to make himself indispensable to his employer. Some valets therefore became possessive of those for whom they worked, controlling access to them, running their lives, and putting off those – including old friends and relations – they did not like. On the whole, however, these were efficient men who gained a great deal of satisfaction from the work they did. In the series *Downton Abbey*, the young solicitor who finds himself in the position of having the services of a valet thrust upon him is initially resentful. In the opening years of the twentieth century, he sees such a man as unnecessary and even as a hindrance. He gives his valet nothing to do because he is able to dress himself and look after his own clothes. Only when it is pointed out to him how unfair this is to his valet does it dawn on him that the master-servant relationship is a two-way one. It is a matter of professional pride to a good manservant that he should work hard in his apparently servile position. It is unkind and thoughtless, as well as wasteful, to ignore the professional expertise of a skilled servant.

Though one might expect a valet to be appreciated by his master, life could be extremely difficult if the man were cantankerous or demanding, and it was not unheard of for a put-upon servant to retaliate. In 1840, the irascible Lord William Russell, uncle of the Prime Minister, was murdered one night by his Swiss valet, François Courvoisier. Public opinion was strongly against the valet. He was seen not as having finally snapped after innumerable provocations but as having betrayed the trust of someone who was entirely at his mercy, sleeping unprotected in the same house. He was hanged in public, a spectacle witnessed by Charles Dickens whose own grandfather had worked as a footman in a grand household.

Footmen were known by their Christian names, although these would commonly be changed by their employers. There might be a tradition of using certain names in a household, and this practice offered continuity. In the series *Upstairs, Downstairs* the Scottish butler was named Angus Hudson. When he had begun his career in service as a footman to the Earl of Southwold, he had been told that he would henceforth be addressed as Charles. Not only would this have been the traditional name for such servants, it was also important that it should be short and uncomplicated, easy for visitors – including foreign ones – to remember and to pronounce. Once he became a butler, he was of course never again addressed by his Christian name.

It was the footmen's task to lay the cloth before meals and to put out the cutlery under the supervision of the butler. Sartorially, these men were the elite of the servant world. They were the most splendidly dressed, for even their superior, the butler, did not wear livery but a black tailcoat. Their other duties were often light, and the men themselves seemed primarily concerned with not doing anything that would dirty their livery, which was in any case the property of their employer. Standing posturing in hallways and corridors for hours each day, they were often seen as haughty, full of themselves and sexually predatory, and in spite of their lack of gallantry in refusing to assist with the heavy work, they often set hearts fluttering among the female staff. If they worked in a great house, footmen would have several liveries, or at least separate ones for morning and evening. While in daytime they might wear a cutaway tailcoat of some uniform colour with brass buttons and black trousers, they would have to look more elaborate on formal occasions, whether this were a ball or banquet or one of the outside visits with their mistress in her carriage. Their colourful 'state livery' would include a brightly coloured tailcoat with decorative lace and probably a gold aiguillette attached to one shoulder, They would have waistcoats and knee breeches of plush or silk, and buckled, patent-leather pumps. There would also be white cotton gloves and, for outdoor wear, a bicorne hat, perhaps with gold decoration.

Their hair had to be powdered for great occasions, covered in a mixture of baking soda, soap and water and left to stiffen. One cannot help feeling that a wig would have looked more impressive as well as being much more convenient. Hair powder took a long time to mix and put on. It made a considerable mess, smelled unpleasant, and because it had to be applied while damp, caused numerous head colds among those who had to stand about in draughty halls or on the backs of carriages in this state. Royal servants – for the Royal Household has tended to be the last place in which many of these aristocratic customs still persist – continued to powder their hair until the 1950s, when the Duke of Edinburgh had the practice discontinued.

Footmen were required to be tall. With a large pool of manpower to call upon, Victorians sought men for these posts who were over five feet six inches. This does not count as 'tall' by today's standards, but it remained a benchmark for many years. Applicants for positions as footmen were paid significantly more if they were in excess of this height – in fact it was worth almost an additional £10 a year to be over five feet ten inches. It was also an advantage to be handsome. In the decades when large side-whiskers were habitual for men, footmen often grew theirs to impressive proportions, to add to the dignity of their appearance.

One reason for employers' insistence on hiring men of a particular size was that livery was already made – it was passed down from one employee to another – and could not be cut down to fit a smaller figure without ruining the elaborate decoration. The man, therefore, had to fit the uniform rather than the other way round. In a historical novel set in Victorian times, Peter Carey's *Jack Maggs*, a footman is required to wear not only the livery but the patent leather pumps of his smaller predecessor, which, as painful as it sounds, must also have happened in reality.

In the grandest houses, which were considered the most desirable places to work, footmen would commonly be well over six feet tall. Their employers would seek to match them in pairs, in much the same way as they did their carriage horses, for it was regarded as highly impressive to have two giants of exactly the same height – or half a dozen of them, for that matter. The impressive physique they were expected to display included shapely calves, which were especially noticeable because of the knee breeches they wore. Where nature had not been sufficiently kind, they wore false calves made from cork (this was also common practice among actors on stage), and it caused much ribaldry among small boys in the street if a hapless footman's 'calf' slipped as he was walking along. Indeed the pompous footman was a figure of fun to music-hall audiences and the readers of the satirical press, for his overblown appearance and sneering expression simply invited ridicule when out in public he could expect to be subject to catcalls from urchins, and very possibly stones or other missiles intended to dirty his livery. This would, however, happen only in town, never in the country. The footman whose livery was recognized by passers-by and trades-men in a local market town, and was known to be from the big house, could expect the same deference as was shown to his master.

Footmen had to wash the silver every day, a task that took up much of their time when they were not upstairs waiting in the hall. It was wiped with a cloth of soft leather, and had to be polished as well, about once a week, with a paste made from hartshorn powder.

These servants, like the grooms and coachman, accom-panied their mistress on shopping trips, and were a common sight in Regent Street or Bond Street, standing in groups outside the stores, waiting to carry parcels out to the carriage. This was a rare opportunity for them to meet and spend time in conversation with their counterparts from other households, and the air of colour and dignity brought to the pavements by their liveries was much admired.

There was hierarchy even in the nursery, where the son and heir was looked after by the nanny and the other children by more junior nursery maids. The food in the nursery was plain but considered adequately wholesome, and walks were usually a form of outdoor play that enabled the children to let off steam. As we have seen, sometimes a child would have a footman assigned to them and this man would become their playmate or mentor.

Nannies were usually regarded with affection by their charges, both during childhood and afterwards, and might serve the family for several generations. They tended therefore to become repositories of family and general lore, and could comfort children with tales of how their parents had been equally mischievous. Traditionally the children would seek knowledge and even companionship from these nursery servants. They also had their lessons together until the age of eleven or so. The boys then went off to school, while their sisters remained at home.

Parlourmaids and chambermaids were separate entities, 'tweenies' or between-stairs maids were neither one nor the other, and carried out the functions of both. Parlour maids dealt exclusively with the 'public' rooms of the house – the drawing room, dining room, morning room, library. Their function was to clean carpets and grates, and to polish furniture. Chambermaids dealt with the bedrooms; as well as keeping these clean, they were the people who carried hot water up the backstairs to family and guests, as well as bringing their morning tea and opening the curtains. They were the most visible among the lower servants, and therefore the ones who most often received tips from visitors.

Every estate would have its own carpenter. He would have made furniture for the servants' hall, as well as for the garden. He would probably also have made toys for the children of the house. There might well be an upholsterer too to undertake repairs to furniture. There could be a blacksmith to keep the estate horses shod but also to make iron tyres for horse-drawn vehicles as well as items of decorative ironwork. Out of doors there would be gardeners, gamekeepers and foresters. Coachmen and grooms slept above the stables to be near their charges, and were often in close proximity to the outside laundry, where the maids, according to popular legend, were particularly flirtatious.

The staff outdoors would have to be as large as that inside, for in the days before motorized lawnmowers the upkeep of gardens, parks and grounds would be as labour-intensive as any other aspect of country-house work. A glance at any census return from before the First World War will show how many men were employed as gardeners, or gardeners' boys, on estates. Grass was cut by scythe or – where the lawns were big enough – by horse-drawn mowers. Flower beds had to be dug and planted, hedges trimmed, kitchen gardens and hothouses tended, for these filled an important role in feeding the household. The work that today could be done by one or two people with mechanical help would have required fifteen or twenty a hundred years ago.

The head gardener, who like the butler was at the top of his profession, was a man of very considerable skill and knowledge, and in a very few cases this could enable him to transcend the place he worked or the class to which he belonged. As has been seen, Joseph Paxton, who was employed by the Duke of Devonshire at Chatsworth, created a greenhouse there that led to the design of London's Crystal Palace. Paxton became a national celebrity and was knighted by Queen Victoria.

Cleaning was a physically demanding task. To clean a carpet, for instance, meant scattering it with tea leaves and then sweeping them up on hands and knees. Much worse was cleaning the kitchen range, which had to be done first thing each morning before the fire could be set. It had to be blacked first, using a block of black lead. Bits of this were broken off, mixed with water and then brushed on to the grate. The housemaid would keep such implements in her housemaid's box, a tool kit that went everywhere with her. It contained several brushes specific to this task – one for blacking and one for polishing, as well as leathers and cloths and emery paper for general cleaning. Pots and pans had to be scoured using a mixture of sand, salt, flour and vinegar. The laundry took all week, not only because the community was large but because the amount of clothing worn by all classes was greater, and fussier, than it would be in later decades.

On the first day of the week, household washing was sorted into five piles and left to soak in warm water overnight. On Tuesday they would be attacked for the first time, to remove all stains by scrubbing in hot water. This was done with yellow soap and soda crystals. After rinsing, the items would be inspected to ensure that the stains had gone. If not, they would be dealt with again. The traditional remedies were alcohol (for grass stains), kerosene (for blood), chalk (for grease). Whites were bleached with lemon juice.

On Wednesday, washing would be hung out to dry, either in the open air or in drying rooms. From then on the processes included starching, mangling and ironing. Starching required a paste made from flour and water, and was applied to collars, cuffs, aprons and linen. Mangling would go on for hours, as the big sheets and aprons were passed between rollers to squeeze the water out of them. They would then be dried and put into a linen press. Ironing too was laborious, for the weight of the instrument itself was several pounds, and it was heated on a stand next to the fire. Two or three irons would be kept going at once because as each was used it would lose heat and there always had to be another heating up to replace it.

The hours worked by servants were extremely long, and this was proving to be the biggest deterrent to people entering the profession. By the very nature of what they did, servants had to be at work both early and late. The only time it was possible to clean the house was before the family had come down in the mornings, and therefore the staff had to be up and busy by about six o'clock. Some of them, such as the lamp boy, who cleaned all the boots, might have been busy for some time already. The grates had to be cleaned and new fires laid. Carpets had to be swept, surfaces dusted, furniture polished, and all without making so much noise that the family were disturbed (it would not have been possible to use a vacuum cleaner under these circumstances). At the same time a host of other things had to be in progress. Morning tea was being prepared for those upstairs. Breakfast had to be produced. Though the house was quiet during this time, it was humming with activity.

First up in the morning were the scullery and kitchen maids. They had to get the kitchen range lit and the floor cleaned. The hallboy or lamp boy – their duties were similar and their titles therefore used more or less interchangeably to mean the youngest male servant – was the only other person as busy as they were. He had to ensure that there was enough coal or firewood to last the house for the day, as well as cleaning shoes for both servants and for many of the guests.

By seven, the housekeeper and lady's maid would have had their tea brought in by housemaids who were also now at work. The butler would have gone through the house opening the shutters and doors. The housemaids would work their way through the rooms, cleaning the grates and lighting fires in them. They would dust and sweep. In the kitchen, any remaining dish-washing, left from the night before, would be dealt with.

During the next hour, food would be assembled for the day's meals. It would be now that deliveries would start to come in from the estate gardens and from local tradesmen. The servants would be having their breakfast, the table having been laid by the hallboy. As soon as this was finished, the footmen would go to lay the table upstairs for the family's breakfast. The valet and lady's maid would then go to see to the needs of their master and mistress.

At about half-past eight there would be family prayers for which family and servants would assemble, in whatever was the largest room. These would last only a few minutes – the servants would have had their breakfast but the family would not, so they would not wish to linger. Nevertheless, this assembly of the entire household would be considered a useful opportunity for them to inspect the servants' dress and to make any announcements regarding the day's events. The mistress might receive the cook immediately afterwards to discuss the day's menus. At the same time the butler would be with the master for a similar meeting. The kitchen maids would have rushed back downstairs to bring up the family's breakfast.

When this repast was over, the tables must be cleared and all the washing-up dealt with. Since the bedrooms were now empty, they became the next focus of the servants' attentions. They would be cleaned, and the laundry done.

By mid-morning, preparations for luncheon would be well under way. With so many people to feed – servants, family and guests could easily number sixty or so – the process was extremely time-consuming. Knives would have to be sharpened (by the hallboy) and cutlery polished (by the footmen).

At midday the servants, who perhaps had a short break an hour or so earlier, would sit down to lunch. This was also the time at which the children in the nursery would take their meal. All the attention of the kitchen servants would need to be on the dining room for the main luncheon, served at one o'clock. The butler would preside and carve any meat. The leftovers would go to the servants. The clearing and washing of all the dishes afterwards would take some time.

Once that was over the servants would have a respite. The cook would already be baking for tea, but there would be no cleaning to do at this time – and that was the single biggest blessing for the maids. The footmen would have gone out with their mistress or, if she was expecting callers, they, and the butler, would be waiting upstairs to receive them. The lady's maid would have been kept busy dressing her mistress for whatever the afternoon's social events were to be.

Five o'clock was the time established by custom for tea though, in many households, it would take place at four, served in the drawing room, or perhaps out of doors if the weather permitted. Preparations would already be under way for dinner. The same round of vegetable peeling and water-heating would be going on as took place in the morning. The servants would have their evening meal at about half-past five, eating before they served just as restaurant staff do today. The footmen would lay the table upstairs and the butler would inspect everything. Dinner might be of anything from five to eight courses. The butler would, of course, also have decanted the wine.

At seven, the ladies would go upstairs to bathe and dress formally, attended by their maids. This would be a brief interlude only, for dinner would be served at eight, yet ladies would have their hair brushed and styled. A gong would have been sounded as the signal to both men and women to retire to their rooms to dress, and another would announce that the meal was ready. When they arrived in the dining room they would find the first course awaiting them.

Downstairs, the servants would have their own supper once the fetching and carrying for those upstairs was finished, so that both parties would for once in the day be eating at the same time. Again, this interlude would not be lengthy, for the dining table would have to be cleared and the washing of dishes performed again. By about ten o'clock the room would be empty because the ladies would have retired to the drawing room and the men to the smoking room or library. By ten o'clock also the servants would normally be in bed if they had no remaining duties.

The cook and housekeeper, having made sure that the final chores were done, could retire, provided there was no further demand for anything to eat. The butler had to stay up until everyone else had gone upstairs because he had the responsibility for locking all doors and windows and of making sure fires were not left burning. He might have to get by on only a few hours' sleep, since he would have to be up very early the next morning.

Dinner was the most important meal of the day upstairs, and was conducted formally no matter how few diners there were. People always dressed up for it, and silver would be used. It would consist of five or six courses at least, with more during a dinner party. The butler carved, and footmen served, offering vegetables separately to each diner. Any other servant could also be roped in to help, though coach-house staff had to lose all stable smells beforehand.

It would be usual for a hostess to hold a dinner party twice a week, though this was more the case in town than in the country, where suitable guests were less numerous. The leftovers would, as usual, be devoured by the servants the next day. The additional staff who were sometimes required for larger entertainments were brought in from restaurants or other outside businesses, but were generally thought to be unsatisfactory. The best supplementary staff were 'servants out of place', who would know how to behave properly. A butler would usually have enough professional contacts to find suitable young men. Dinner parties were planned about three weeks ahead.

Guests would be invited that far ahead (it was later to become five or six weeks) and a reply would be expected at once. The guests would arrive fifteen minutes before the time stated. Footmen would take their coats and the butler would announce their arrival in the drawing room, where their hosts would be waiting. Dinner was not served until the last guest had arrived. As usual, the first course would be waiting for them in the dining room. They would go in at eight o'clock, and each man would be paired with a woman. They sat in chairs that were pulled out for them by footmen but their backs never touched these, for they sat bolt upright.

At a dinner such as these eight or ten courses would be served, several of which involved choices, just as they would in a restaurant. Soups were of course the first things brought to the table, and would be served with sherry. The second course would be fish. The entrée would probably be a meat course with cutlets or sweetbreads. This would be followed by the relevée, or main course, which would be meat or poultry. A game course of duck, pheasant or partridge would follow. This was always accompanied by game chips, which were fried potatoes sliced very thin. After this came the ices and desserts, but only once the table had been cleared and laid with fresh cutlery and glasses.

The final course was fruit and nuts, with which port and Madeira arrived. It was at this stage that the ladies retired, to have coffee in the drawing room. The men remained, and were now able to smoke. The butler would continue to hover in case anything further were needed, and the servants would remain on duty until the last guest had either gone home or up to bed, and the hosts had also retired. A good hostess would be concerned that her staff should not be kept out of bed too late. Be this as it may, she would not think of allowing them to sleep late the next morning by way of compensation. The day's tasks had to be performed on time regardless. It would be even more arduous work during the Season, for at balls supper often did not begin until midnight.

With shooting parties there was a similarly early start. Packed luncheon had to be made in readiness, and the kitchen was therefore busy from dawn.

By the end of Victoria's reign, the notion of a household boasting large numbers of costumed and liveried servants was becoming an anachronism. Throughout history the number of servants employed in a great house was viewed as evidence of the owner's prestige, and the sight of men in gorgeous livery standing about the halls and corridors, was intended to impress visitors while at the same time swelling the ranks of the servants' hall. By the beginning of the twentieth century, however, there was no need for such men. The telephone and the servants' bell had made part of their function redundant, and there was in any case a sense of make-believe or pantomime about the use of uniformed servants by those whose own status or background lay outside the traditional aristocracy, with no previous history of employing footmen. If your family had had such servants for generations you could be forgiven for merely carrying on custom. In *parvenus* the practice was considered risible. There was no reason, no excuse, for such ostentation, especially when the general public was as aware as the aristocracy itself that the heyday of this way of life was passing.

Many contemporary commentators were conscious that the age of the true aristocracy had ended and the new era of the self-made man had dawned. Frederick Willis, a hatter who had no connection with either the landowning class or the servant one, was to recall more than fifty years later that:

> The new plutocracy was making [a] tremendous display of flunkeydom. Footmen were a part of a gentleman's retinue in the eighteenth century; in the twentieth they were an anachronism. The social climbers knew nothing of this. The old country houses were passing into decay, the old landed gentry passing after their long reign, but the new country houses were springing up and new commercial gentry blossoming. Neither they nor their houses were to last for long.

It is a matter of record that the last occasion on which the old aristocracy appeared in London in numbers, complete with coaches, grooms and footmen, was not at a function just before the outbreak of the Great War, but for the coronation of King Edward VII in August 1902, and only then in response to a specific request from the King that they should do so. While the ceremony went on in Westminster Abbey, the carriages and their gorgeously clad attendants waited in nearby Whitehall, a sight that would never be seen again even though there was another coronation – in 1911, for King George V – before the era came to an end.

In other words, even without the intervention of a major war, the old ways were dying out. As living standards had risen, fewer people wanted to be servants. Emigration, actively being propagated by charitable societies and by colonial governments, offered greater inducements and opportunities. Though it must be remembered that a country-house kitchen was a far cleaner, quieter and less dangerous place than a factory, here too conditions were steadily improving and the wages could be tempting. Also, in 1911 legislation made it necessary for servants as well as their employers to pay threepence a week National Insurance. Though this seems an insignificant sum, it quickly added up when it was paid for each member of staff, fifty-two weeks a year (think of the Duke of Westminster's 300 or more servants). It meant that some middle-class houses, even with only a few domestics, could no longer afford to keep them all. The owners of country houses too found that keeping up with the higher wages that domestics now expected was increasingly difficult, and made a bigger dent in the household budget. The revenue they derived from their estates remained the same, and thus they felt squeezed at both ends.

As well as the old-age pension, the government had introduced Unemployment Benefit, and this made some men and women, who could have gone into service, prefer to do nothing. The whole of the servant-keeping class was aware that the initiative was being lost – that it was becoming the domestic and not the householder who would henceforth set the terms. Old-fashioned, willing servants seemed to become rarer all the time.

To counter this, more leisure for servants was gradually introduced. Until the 1880s they had had virtually no time off, though some employers had already by then shown the way in terms of improved conditions. The Duke of Portland, by the 1850s, was already holding a ball for the servants on his estate at Welbeck Abbey. (The ballroom was built underground.) He hired an orchestra and a staff of fifty waiters so that his own household would not have to do any work. He led the first dance with the housekeeper while his wife led off with the steward. The 'upstairs family' made a point of leaving at midnight so that the servants could let their hair down.

By the beginning of the twentieth century, servants' conditions had improved to the extent that it was now more or less universally accepted that they were given presents at Christmas that might be worth the equivalent of several weeks' pay. Male servants were likely to receive cash while females were given dressmaking material.

By 1900 the notion of a half-day off every week had become widely accepted. What was also widely expected, however, was that the servant's free time could only begin once their set tasks had been completed. If they were required at the last minute to do something, their liberty would simply be postponed, for there was no question of being able to take 'time off in lieu'. Servants were also subject to a curfew, which was normally eight o'clock for juniors and nine for the older ones. If they failed to return by that time they could expect to be locked out. The housekeeper was nominally in charge of ensuring that the maids returned on time, though she might well delegate the task of letting them in to one of their colleagues. Servants could find themselves – and this is likely to have been very common – too tired to go out on a day off anyway. Given the lack of sleep that many experienced, they might simply have wanted to put their heads down as soon as they had the opportunity.

In addition, servants whose families lived some distance away might be allowed by a sympathetic employer to save up days off until there were enough to cover a visit there. By the early twentieth century it was in any case becoming standard for servants to have a week's paid holiday, taken at a time of year – usually in the quieter weeks of the summer – that was convenient to the employer. This was something for which servants saved up over the long months beforehand – the train fare, after all, would be expensive even by Third Class if the distance was great.

With the outbreak of hostilities in 1914, the trickle away from domestic service rapidly became a flood. The Great War took over 400,000 servants away to various forms of war work, for many thousands of women departed to take up jobs that men had left vacant. The shorter hours and considerably higher pay that went with this vital war work meant that many – probably most – such people were extremely reluctant to re-enter the life of servitude they had once led. The wages young women could earn in factory jobs seemed fantastic by the standards of their class, enabling them to dress like their employers.

It was being brought home to the servant-keeping class that their needs could no longer come first: it was now a question of patriotism. *Country Life* published an advertisement during 1915 that read: 'Have you a Butler, Groom, Chauffeur, Gardener or Gamekeeper serving you who, at this moment, should be serving your king and country? Have you men preserving your game who should be preserving your country?'

Among young girls, whether they had previously been in service or not, there was an obvious and intense dislike of the very notion of service. It was completely 'out of fashion', and the problem of filling the places left vacant would become more and more difficult to solve (in fact, it would prove impossible).

In some respects, however, the experience of war encouraged both masters and servants to see each other differently. Those of the gentry who had served in it were far less inclined afterwards to view their staff as mere automata, and those below stairs had experienced during hostilities an unexpected and previously un-known sense of camaraderie and relative equality with their officers. Even among those who had stayed at home there was a different mindset thanks to the changes wrought by the war. Highclere Castle in Hampshire was used – like numerous other country houses – as a military hospital. It was run in person by the Countess of Carnarvon, assisted by her maids and footmen, who acted as medical orderlies. In this situation too there was a sense of camaraderie – perhaps unacknowledged but definitely there – between employer and servants. This sort of shared experience produced, at the very least, a greater mutual understanding.

Once the war was over, the number of girls considering service was so reduced that training colleges were set up to try and develop a sense of pride and efficiency in household work. These attracted applicants, but they did not succeed in stemming the tide of sheer disinclination to practise these skills as a servant. Nothing about such a prospect appealed to them, even if (especially if!) their family had been in service before. Opportunities in factories, shops, cafés and restaurants were simply too common and too promising to miss, and women especially preferred these because the hours were much shorter and there was far more personal freedom. The wages offered in both the private and public sectors increased sharply. The concessions offered by employers of servants had to become increasingly generous.

Employers, who tended to swallow the myth that servants were happy with their lot and grateful for the positions they held, sometimes felt betrayed that the posts they had held open during the period of hostilities were not wanted when their former staff returned from war service. They resented the fact that servants now made demands on them, expecting privileges that seemed frankly unreasonable. When Rose Plummer went to be interviewed for a new position, she stated that she wanted not only higher wages than the prospective mistress was willing to pay, but a regular amount of time off that was seen as outrageous. The employer's reaction was to exclaim that if Miss Plummer had such privileges, all the other staff would want them – the clear implication being that anarchy would result. (Nevertheless she granted both requests.)

Not since the Black Death in the fourteenth century had wiped out thousands of labourers and made the survivors a sought-after rarity had the servant class been able to exert such dominance. Their would-be employers, who had grown up in households filled with domestic staff and had never had to cook or clean for themselves, often lacked the most basic notions of how to do these things. Where they were dependent upon servants to run their household and could not rely on family retainers who stayed with them out of sentiment, they had to sacrifice both money and dignity in order to keep them.

As the general disinclination to work in service gathered pace, good servants became scarcer, better appreciated, ever-more demanding. For a further generation, until the coming of the next war, the country houses managed to keep at least the appearance that they were continuing their way of life largely unchanged. The economic slump of the twenties and the ensuing scarcity of manufacturing work would have helped to repopulate the servants' halls to some extent, though there was nothing like a return to the pre-1914 numbers. After the Second World War, of course, there could no longer be any such pretence. The era of the country house was over.

A passage in Evelyn Waugh's novel *Decline and Fall*, published in 1928, gives a glimpse of the new social climate in great houses. King's Thursday is the family home of the Beste-Chetwyndes, Earls of Pastmaster. Built in Tudor times, it has never been altered or added to since – there is no plumbing or electricity, and its unspoiled quaintness is much admired by visitors. However, the family discover that the charms of Tudor interiors are not appreciated by their staff, who do not choose to remain, for:

> [T]he bedrooms obtained for them among the rafters were unsuited to modern requirements, and only the dirtiest and most tipsy of cooks could be induced to inhabit the kitchen. Housemaids tended to melt away under the strain of trotting before breakfast up the narrow servants' staircases and along the interminable passages with jugs of warm water. Modern democracy called for lifts and labour-saving devices, for hot-water taps and cold-water taps, gas-rings and electric ovens.

This provides a fitting epitaph for the age of the servant – they were still there, and they would remain for a few further years, but their new conditions of work bore little resemblance to those of their forelock-tugging predecessors. Within a few more years they would, for most householders, be an unaffordable and unattainable luxury.

# EPILOGUE: THE PEOPLE

The life lived by the 'upstairs' folk – insofar as it was a formal, codified way of giving and receiving visits – came to an end as soon as the Second World War began. It had been increasingly obvious since Hitler came to power in 1933 that another European conflict was likely. By 1938, when Britain and France gave in to the dictator's demands over the subjugation of Czechoslovakia, it was a certainty. That act of appeasement gave British Society the breathing space to enjoy a final round of aristocratic pleasures in the summer of 1939, but there was a sort of desperate gaiety, a last-days-of-Pompeii atmosphere about the balls and parties. The young men who attended them-knew they would soon be in uniform.

It is difficult, from a later perspective, to appreciate the sense of Armageddon that pervaded the late summer of that year. As war began at the beginning of September, the Season was ending and the great houses were shut for what could well have been the last time. It was widely expected, based on recent memory of the bombing of Guernica in the Spanish Civil War, that massive air-raids could follow in a matter of days. Some people touched the walls or fingered the curtains, taking leave, assuming that within the week the town houses of the aristocracy, and much of London, might literally no longer exist.

There were to be two 'blitzes' rather than one. The first, in 1940–41, was delivered by bombers, the second, in the last year of the war, by unmanned rockets. Damage, though grievous in both town and country, was not as apocalyptic as had been anticipated. Nevertheless the conflict delivered the *coup de grace* to the world of Edwardian hedonism. It brought shortages not only of staff but of food, clothing, petrol and almost everything that made for comfort. Young people, always the mainstay of a country house weekend, would henceforth be in the armed forces and scattered all over the world. Every citizen had at least some nominal duty to perform, and there could not be any pretence of uninterrupted, full-time leisure. All classes shared anxiety about the conduct of the war, whether this meant preparing for enemy invasion or worrying about friends and relatives in danger. Flippancy was out of fashion. Unlike the previous conflict, it was not only the sons of great houses that might become victims, but the very fabric of their homes. Commandeered for official purposes, scores of houses were damaged, if not destroyed, by neglect and by military or official occupation. Once the conflict had ended the specialist labour necessary to repair, replaster or re-roof was hard to find in a country dominated by a severe housing shortage. Gardens that had been dug up for the growing of vegetables could not be returned to lawn overnight. The staff required to keep the household running was perhaps the most difficult thing to obtain. As industry set out to recover, the manufacturing sector was working at full stretch and wages were escalating. Both men and women were even less inclined to go into service than their predecessors had been after the last war. Though some of the very grandest houses could carry on, in most cases the servants' halls were virtually empty. There were too few left to perform the tasks that a country house required, even with the aid of labour-saving technology.

But the owners too had changed. There had been a revolution in their expectations. By the late 1940s the landowning families had already lived through two decades of decline. An entire generation had grown up accustomed to financial hardship and sacrifice. They were used to seeing pictures disappear from their walls and acres sold from their grounds to pay taxes. The outbreak of war in 1939 had then brought nearly six years of much more acute privation and of the need to make do. Sleeping in unheated bedrooms, dining in semi-darkness on rationed food, and doing the cooking themselves were by now routine experiences for many. The whole nation had had to become much tougher, and the upper class followed – indeed had often set an example and led – this trend. The more self-reliant and enterprising of them saw it as a challenge, an adventure, a necessary patriotic duty, for 'doing one's bit' was a national watchword and there was a prevalent feeling that sacrificing peacetime luxuries was of direct benefit to the war-effort. To the owners of country houses, as they dined upon spam or rabbit pie, the ways of their Edwardian forebears will have seemed as wanton and wasteful as they did to other members of society. The notion of being awoken by a servant with an ironed newspaper, commonplace only thirty years earlier, would have been a laughable extravagance.

With this privation, a new era of informality arrived both in country houses and in the world beyond. Clothes could not be as formal because material was difficult to obtain. Schoolboys at Eton ceased to wear the top hat after 1940, partly because it was no longer possible to get them made, and partly because everyone was now required to carry a gas-mask in a satchel over their shoulder, and the putting on of this every day meant that a hat was simply one encumbrance too many. At home the boys' relations, if they were not in uniform, might well be wearing pullovers and Wellington boots around the house instead of tweed suits, frock coats or day dresses. The fact that clothing remained rationed until the early 1950s meant that, even after peace came, there could be no sudden return to pre-war elegance.

As a class, the landowners no longer saw themselves as a race apart. They had shared not only – on the part of men – the dangers of the front line with their former servants, as they had done in the First World War, they had also experienced with other classes the hardships of the Home Front – air-raids, rationing, blackouts, and anxiety over loved ones. British society could not, during those years, be said to consist of 'two nations' (a phrase used by Victorian novelist and Prime Minister Benjamin Disraeli to describe the isolated worlds of rich and poor).

Even the wife of the current Prime Minister, the aristocratic Winston Churchill, made the gesture of wearing in public a hat that was like those of female factory-workers – effectively a simple headscarf tied turban-fashion to keep hair out of the way. This equality was not as universal as national mythology has suggested. number of wealthy families had sent their children – or even gone themselves – to safety in North America at the start of hostilities. Nevertheless there was a sense of common hardship and common purpose that went some way to eroding class differences.

The British public was getting used to equality. Rationing of food meant that, for the first time in history, all classes had access to the same level of nutrition. The poorest were able to eat better than ever before, and the general health of the population rapidly improved. The Government set officials to work on 'post-war planning' long before the conflict actually ended, to design new towns, new schools, new recreational facilities. All of this led to an expectation that once peace came there would be a wealth of change in environment, opportunities and attitudes, and that a more equitable sharing of resources would result. In one field – education – this process had already begun. From 1944, Oxford and Cambridge began recruiting undergraduates from a much wider range of social backgrounds.

Regarding the upper class, the public had developed an increasing impatience. This class, as represented by the pre-war Conservative Government, was roundly blamed for failing to see the war coming and for involving Britain in it. Every reluctant soldier at the front blamed the Conservatives for putting him there, and astute observers were aware that as soon as the electorate had a chance to take revenge they would do so. Though the Government had been a coalition throughout the conflict it contained a number of prominent Conservatives – most conspicuously Churchill himself, whose able leadership would not save him from electoral defeat.

Though a general election did not take place until July 1945 – and result in a landslide victory for the Labour Party – the writing was already on the wall. In the spring of 1944 there was an important by-election at Bakewell in Derbyshire. One of the candidates was the Marquess of Hartington, eldest son of the Duke of Devonshire. Like many aristocrats, the Devonshires had always nominated candidates for the local parliamentary seat and expected the populace to endorse them. On this occasion Hartington, though a man of genuine integrity and ability, was routed by his socialist opponent (a serving soldier, the Marquess was in any case killed in Normandy only a few weeks later). The people of Bakewell were sending a deliberate massage that they would no longer do as their betters expected them to – in some cases, the new era arrived even before the war was over.

The decisive victory of a Labour government brought in an era of nationalisation and equality ('We are the masters now!' yelled one labour M.P. during a debate in the House of Commons – though he would later defect to the Conservatives). The life of the country house patently did not fit with the social and political climate of these times. Though industry was expanding and there was little unemployment, austerity measures still applied to many areas of life and shortages were to remain for years after 1945. The enjoyments of the upper class remained muted for a time.

This feeling did not last long, however. By 1951 the Conservatives were back in power, to remain there until 1964. The country gradually became wealthier, but now there were other perspectives, other priorities. During the '50s, the wages of young people soared in proportion to those of other age groups. This created the 'teenager' as a part of the social landscape – a group whose spending-power deserved respect – and it also put the final nail in the coffin of domestic service as a career for young Britons. Servants, thereafter, would increasingly be recruited from poorer places overseas.

The notion of the political house party, so much a feature of British society from Georgian times onward, had survived the Great War and had flourished through the twenties and thirties ( the great hostesses – Nancy Cunard, Lady Diana Cooper, Lady Astor – were among the major personalities of the day). It lasted until the 1960s. The Prime Minister from 1957-63, Harold Macmillan, was the personification of the old-school English gentleman. He disdained the use of Chequers (the 'stately home' that is the official weekend home of British premiers) because he preferred his own country residence, Birch Grove in Sussex. His successor, Sir Alec Douglas-Home (who happened to be the 14th Earl of Home, a member of an ancient Scottish noble family) was the last Prime Minister to possess his own ancestral country house, but by the time he took on the Premiership scandal had already severed the link between political machinations and manicured parkland.

Cliveden was the country home of the Astors, an imposing house overlooking a bend in the River Thames in rural Berkshire. At a party there in 1961 John Profumo, the Secretary of State for War, met a call-girl named Christine Keeler. They had a brief affair, though he ended it after a few weeks. It was a year before rumours of this reached the public but they provoked widespread outrage, for it transpired that Miss Keeler had also had a close friendship with the Senior Naval Attache at the Soviet Embassy. The risk to national security in an era of international tension (1962 was the year of the Cuban missile crisis) was grave. Profumo, challenged to make a statement in the House of Commons in March 1963, denied that there had been any impropriety. When the truth came out and it was found that he had misled his colleagues he was forced to resign. The Prime Minister's own resignation followed shortly afterward. The Conservative Government limped on for a further year but was then defeated in a general election. Any notion of powerful political figures gathering for relaxation at a country house would from now on be a cause of sniggering speculation and innuendo on the part of press and public.

There were other factors that had already eroded respect for the upper class. In 1951 two young men in sensitive Foreign Office posts, Donald Maclean and Guy Burgess, had defected to Moscow and been revealed as Soviet spies. The information they had given to Stalin's government had caused immense damage to the West. Both had been from highly-educated, socially-influential backgrounds of the sort that were thought to make them automatically suited to the Diplomatic Service, though it had somehow been overlooked that they had had strong communist sympathies while at Cambridge in the thirties. In 1963 another man from the same circle, Kim Philby, also defected to Russia. The public wondered how many more effete young men would turn out to have been traitors. The notion that the upper class had an automatic right to rule because of background, or connections, or inherent understanding of politics and diplomacy was in tatters. That homosexuality had also been involved heaped further fuel on the flames.

And what of upper class women? They too had had to endure scandal, both in fiction and in reality. The book that outsold all others at the beginning of the sixties was *Lady Chatterly's Lover*, a novel written by D.H. Lawrence over thirty years earlier but which had not been available in Britain until it was issued, by Penguin, in 1960. It told the story of a titled lady who had an affair with a gardener on her estate – an unthinkable breach of propriety to members of her class. It was not the subject-matter so much as the treatment of this relationship that caused an official outcry, however. The language and description were earthy and vivid, the sexual encounters rough and animalistic. The four-letter words that littered the text had never before been used in print in 'polite' literature. The result was that Penguin was prosecuted under the Obscene Publications Act. The trial attracted immense public interest and copies of the book (in paperback, and thus affordable) flew off the shelves. The court found in favour of the publisher, opening the floodgates for any others with similar inclinations. Some of those who read the novel may have known that Lawrence had based his plot in part on reality. The literary hostess Lady Ottoline Morrell had allegedly had such a relationship with a man on her estate (a sculptor of garden statuary rather than, in the novel, a gamekeeper). This too went some way to diminishing respect for the 'ruling class' whose opportunities and education, it had been assumed, would place them above such basic behaviour.

If any doubts remained, they were dispelled by the divorce, in 1963, of the Duke and Duchess of Argyll. The Duchess, who as Margaret Whigham had been Debutante of the Year in 1938, was famously beautiful and had been previously married. Such was her sexual voracity that her husband cited an incredible 88 co-respondents, allegedly including government ministers, members of the Royal Family and at least one film star. The country was torn between shame and curiosity as the details emerged.

After the War there was, as we have seen, little left of the institution of domestic service. With so few houses retaining large staffs, the hierarchy that had seemed so impregnable within living memory was obsolete and unsustainable. Stewards, under-butlers and footmen disappeared, as did the 'pugs' parlour' and the notion of senior and junior servants. Though the maid, always the most common type of domestic, remained, the 'housekeeper' – formerly a specific title for the most senior woman below stairs, and a word that inspired considerable respect – had become a loose term for a general female servant who might be little more than a daily cleaning woman, and who could well be the only domestic on the premises. She might combine cooking with her cleaning work, and ironically thus became a latter-day version of that Victorian stock-character, the maid-of-all-work. Such was the change in both circumstances and attitudes, however, that she was often treated from the beginning as a member of the family, and her employers would take it for granted that they had to do their own cooking when it was her weekly night off.

Though the 'downstairs' side of country house life thus became all but extinct, the 'upstairs' has survived largely intact, if not in the full glory of its golden age then at least in the rituals and the institutions that make up the life of the upper class. The annual round of rural events goes on as it always has, and with undiminished popularity. There are still garden parties on the lawns of country houses. There are still village fetes at which aristocrats present the prizes. There are cricket matches, point-to-points, horse-trials. Packs of hounds, and galloping horsemen, still bring colour to the winter countryside even though the Government made foxhunting illegal a few years ago, for the hunts still meet and go through the motions – it is just that the fox is no longer killed by the hounds. In one indication that the 'posh' are becoming even posher, polo – an expensive game that requires each player to have a string of ponies – has become widespread at public schools, not one of whom boasted a team a generation ago. The upper class, for all its troubled recent history, is not in hiding and is still able to go about its business with vigour and enthusiasm. There is, in the Country Landowners' Association, a professional body for those who oversee estates.

Like their forms of leisure, the institutions of British Society go on as before. No revolution has overthrown them, no force – political, social or economic – has proved strong enough to remove or even to seriously challenge them. The public schools, the training ground of Britain's social elite, flourish today as they did in the reign of Victoria. Some have closed, or merged, as a result of changing fashion or difficulty in keeping financially afloat, but new ones have also opened. Because their teaching and facilities are often excellent, they remain fully subscribed and highly respected even in a meritocratic age. The ancient universities of Oxford and Cambridge, now much more intellectually selective than in the days when aristocrats merely had to choose to attend, have shut out a large percentage of upper class youth. These have responded by colonising other seats of learning, giving to some universities a reputation for parties, debutantes and field sports that they did not have even a decade or two previously.

The 'smart' regiments of the British Army continue to recruit officers from top-drawer backgrounds. A Guards officer today is as gorgeously dressed, and as aristocratic, as he would have been in the reign of Edward VII, though the studied languor will now conceal a thorough professionalism and a familiarity with modern weaponry. The young woman he marries will normally be his female counterpart – privately educated, polished in speech and behaviour, linked by blood or school or merely by party-circuit with a host of similar people, part of a network that remains vigorously alive.

Even the Season continues. It is much less conspicuous than before 1939, because it commands far less media attention. The grand town houses of the aristocracy have almost all gone, and therefore the balls that once provided set-piece occasions for the launch of young women into the world have been replaced by more informal cocktail parties, perhaps at one of the gentlemen's clubs. Presentations at Court were discontinued in 1957, though the impetus came not from any Labour government but from the Queen, for the event served no useful purpose and could be a chore for all those involved. Debutantes no longer traipse past the monarch, though they do still study the social graces. Young women continue to 'come out', though those that do are often the daughters of international businessmen rather than aristocrats, and the events they attend owe a good deal to corporate sponsors. Queen Charlotte's Ball, first held in 1780 for the wife of George III, still takes place as a charity fundraising event. Instead of sinking in practiced curtsies to a sovereign, the girls bend the knee toward a giant cake, the successor to the one with which Queen Charlotte celebrated. For young women of patrician background, whose families are confident enough of their social standing not to need the endorsement of formal ceremony university, or 'gap year' foreign travel, provide a more practical and enjoyable introduction to the world.

The shops and the clubs patronised by the aristocracy, the tailors and hatters and gunsmiths, are still doing business, as expensive and exclusive today as ever. There are no circumstances foreseeable in which, in this aspect at least, the world of Downton is going to end within our lifetime.

# EPILOGUE: THE HOUSES

*The State Apartments keep their historical renown,*
*It's wiser not to sleep there, in case they tumble down;*
*But still, if they ever catch on fire*
*Which, with any luck, they might,*
*We'll fight for the Stately Homes of England.*
  Noël Coward, 'The Stately Homes of England', 1926

'It is a fact, patent to all and deplored by some, that the large-scale private paradise is already obsolescent.'
                                        Clough Williams-Ellis

'What country houses of any size, one wonders, can hope to survive the next fifty years?'
                                        Osbert Sitwell

For almost a century the great houses of Britain have been in decline, suffering from crippling maintenance costs, taxation, the difficulties of staffing them, and even the trend towards smaller families, which naturally produces fewer heirs and family members who can help. As we have seen, one significant blow was the loss of so many young men in the First World War. The heirs to many estates perished in the mud of Flanders and left their parents with little incentive to keep the houses going, as was the case with Castle Drogo, where the building was not even complete when its owner's eldest son was killed.

Perhaps the most poignant reminder of this sacrifice is a plaque in the cloisters at Eton College that commemorates the Grenfell family. Listed on it are the names of seven young men who died in Britain's wars. Of these, one was killed in the Matabele War (1896) and another, two years later, in the famous cavalry charge at Omdurman. A third died of fever while serving in India. The other four were lost in the Great War, three of them in the same place – Ypres – and at the same time, the summer of 1915. Between them they won a DSO and a VC, but this will have brought scant comfort to their surviving relatives. The family home, Wilton Park in the nearby town of Beaconsfield, was left with no heir. It eventually passed into the hands of the Army, who in the 1960s demolished the Regency house, filled in its ornamental lake and now run a language school there.

No one could possibly pretend that the twentieth century, or indeed the present one, represents in any sense a 'golden age' for the English country house, or for those who live in them. However agreeable it is to dwell among beautiful architecture and museum-quality artefacts, many owners faced, and continue to face, a continuous struggle to keep their heads above water financially. Great houses were still being built up to the First World War, and even beyond. Yet Noël Coward's song, written in the 1920s, reflects a situation that was already painfully true for many owners – that of selling paintings by the row, surviving with primitive and broken plumbing, and even hoping that a wing of the house would burn down so that insurance could be claimed. The rot had set in with the collapse of agriculture in the 1870s, and the situation grew worse with the introduction of new forms of taxation. In other words, four or five generations of a landed family may have been fighting a rearguard action to protect their heritage, and this state of affairs will be all they will ever have known.

It was quite obvious to observers by the end of the Great War that the country house no longer had a long life expectancy. So much was now conspiring against it, but principally the combination of greatly increased taxation with greatly reduced land values. The owners simply could not win. Taxation was a more serious threat that at any time in the past. Estate duties, already a generation old (they had begun in 1894), went up to 40 per cent in 1919 on estates worth more than £2 million. Rates and taxes were, by the 1920s, taking on average 30 per cent of the rentals paid to estates. Six million acres were sold throughout the country. As the great houses struggled, the suburbs expanded, swallowing up thousands of acres of agricultural land, and speculators were often waiting to buy any real estate that a family could not afford to maintain. Many country houses were pulled down and their land built upon. These were the blackest days that the owners of such houses had ever faced. They were worse than the troubles caused by agricultural decline fifty years earlier or the economic crises of later decades. It was not just the loss of land or of architectural heritage that was causing such concern, it was the sale of the houses' contents, at a time when regulations on the export of art objects were a great deal less strict. There was little to stop the large-scale removal from the United Kingdom of whole libraries, picture galleries, furnishings and interior fittings.

A collector like William Randolph Hearst (1863–1951), the American newspaper magnate, or Henry E. Huntington, the railway millionaire who collected entire British libraries in his California home, had a virtually limitless budget. If Hearst could – as he did – buy a Spanish monastic cloister to surround his swimming pool in California, it was clear that he and others like him could carry off an important part of Britain's heritage. The country-house owners, and their allies in the British art and museum worlds, felt that it was best to leave these things where possible in their original context, and to have them cared for by those families that had commissioned them and owned them for centuries.

It is ironic that it is precisely this time of decline, dispersal and deep anxiety that seems, from a later perspective, to be such a 'golden age' in country-house life. These were the years recorded in the works of Agatha Christie, Dorothy L. Sayers, P. G. Wodehouse and dozens of other writers. Society still looked up to the aristocracy, and their houses continued to be viewed both as an ideal way of life and an unchanging one, despite the often grim reality. This is the world that evokes such nostalgia when viewed through the camera lens in *Downton Abbey* or *The Remains of the Day*. Yet, however gorgeous the clothes and cars and ladies' hats may have looked, it was a time of the deepest anxiety. Like every other golden age, it would not have seemed golden to those who lived through it.

It was argued that taxation – and estate duty in particular – represented nothing less than a death sentence for many stately homes. If the government could be persuaded that these architectural and antiquarian treasure troves would best serve the nation by being maintained in situ by their owners, these men and women should be assisted through relief from taxation: houses deemed – after examination – to be worthy of preservation with their contents should be made exempt, so long as they were preserved with their collections intact and no attempt was made to sell off valuable items.

It was at this dire moment in the history of the landowning class that a solution was suggested. The beleaguered owners should band together, forming an association of house owners – a trade union, as it were. Like all professional associations they could share expertise, discuss problems and lobby the government. It was not only the owners of estates who rallied to this banner. They had sympathizers in Parliament, in the fields of academia and museum curating, and in the wider public for anyone who appreciated art or valued such collections was likely to share the concern that irreplaceable items might be lost abroad.

Somewhat by default, the National Trust became the focus for this campaign, the organization that came to the rescue of a number of houses and provided an official voice for the landowning class. It had originally been pledged by its founders to the preservation of 'places of historic interest and natural beauty', but much of its work in its early decades had dealt with the natural world – landscape and coasts – rather than the works of man. Nevertheless, it already had in its care two houses in the county of Somerset, Barrington Court and Montacute.

In 1934 one aristocratic owner, the 11th Marquess of Lothian (a man who had inherited not from his father but from a distant cousin, and who had felt the heavy weight of estate duty), made the suggestion that the National Trust should formally extend its remit to encompass the care of historic houses. In a memorable speech he sought to remind the public of the aesthetic and artistic value that these added to the nation's heritage: 'The country houses of Britain with their gardens, their parks, their pictures, their furniture and peculiar architectural charm, represent a quiet beauty which is not only specially characteristic but quite unrivalled in any other land.'

The Society for the Protection of Ancient Buildings was already in existence, but seemed the wrong body to take on, or offer sponsorship or protection to, houses that might well be attached to great acreages of land. This was not a welcome prospect for an organization that needed all its resources to help scores of often small and vulnerable buildings. The Council for the Preservation of Rural England was likewise interested in land but did not necessarily have the time for, or see the relevance of, caring for architectural treasures. It was eventually deemed feasible for the National Trust to take on houses provided they came with sufficient land – or some other form of endowment – to pay for their upkeep, for without the taxes that were levied on private owners, many of these estates became profitable again. The Trust could even pay for renovation and modernization, and – where no family any longer inhabited a house – look for tenants to whom they could be leased. For those owners who wished to remain in their ancestral homes, there would be an uncomfortable adjustment to make – they were no longer able to do exactly as they liked. The organization that would now own the rooms in which they lived would be able to tell them what they were, or were not, allowed to hang on the walls.

The Trust, after a good deal of thought, agreed to accept this responsibility, were its resources adequate to do so, and thus came to take charge of a significant aspect of Britain's heritage. It set up a Historic Country Houses Committee, under the chairmanship of James Lees-Milne. The first property it acquired under this scheme was Lothian's own house, the splendid Blickling Hall in Norfolk. The benefit of the scheme, as one relieved owner wrote in *The Times*, was that it ' . . . combines freedom from responsibilities with the assurance that the connection with the family seat will not be sharply and completely broken'. For those who would visit there was: 'access to treasures of natural and artistic beauty with the preservation of the character which makes the difference between a dwelling and a museum'.

The outcome was two Acts of Parliament – the National Trust Acts of 1937 and 1939 – which launched the Country Houses Scheme. These came just in time. At the end of a deeply troubled period for owners, and on the cusp of a World War that would wreak terrible damage on country houses throughout Britain, the 'stately homes of England' at last had a degree of protection, with the legislation and machinery in place to save them and their contents. It would not be able to help in every case, but it was certainly an excellent beginning, the start of a process that would ultimately bring over 200 such houses within the Trust's stewardship. Several notable properties, representing some of the most-visited houses – West Wycombe Park and Speke Hall, for instance – were donated to the Trust during the conflict, and thus the work of preservation went on even at a time of national danger. Scotland and Northern Ireland, which have always had their own National Trusts, were to follow England's lead and seek to preserve some of their own great houses through similar means.

With the coming of peace in 1945 the future of British stately homes was given a fillip by a new scheme. The government and the public were interested in ways of honouring those who had died in the war, and one outcome was the setting up of the National Land Fund. Launched in 1946 for the purpose of buying property to preserve, it was the work of Clement Attlee, the Prime Minister, and Hugh Dalton, his Chancellor of the Exchequer. These men personified a government that landowners had dreaded – the Labour Party, which had won a sweeping victory in 1945 and was seen as threatening the whole fabric of traditional Britain. In fact, the Fund had the opposite effect – that of enabling many owners to stay in the houses their families had inhabited for generations. It was a generous and far-sighted move by a government that could easily have acted otherwise. The biggest social problem facing the whole country at the time was, after all, the housing shortage.

Since the low point between the wars, several things have helped those who inhabit such properties. There is now a range of government grants available, and the value of land has risen. After generations of fighting a rearguard action, owners have adapted to circumstances, and have often been ingenious in finding other sources of income. To avoid inheritance tax, for instance, an owner will often pass the house on to his heir before his death, thus shifting the burden to the next generation and allowing himself the prospect of retirement.

The future, in a country seemingly obsessed with leisure and dismissed by some critics as a 'historical theme park' is in making the houses – or rather their grounds – fun to visit. Knebworth's Dinosaur Trail is simply one of many visitor attractions that can make a country house more like Legoland than the British Museum. This notion has been taken to extremes at one house, the no-longer-inhabited Alton Towers in Staffordshire. Such fairground attractions are unarguably vulgar, but they can always be dismantled by future generations if fashions change or wealth increases, and if they have enabled historic houses to survive in a difficult economic climate, the sacrifice of some dignity will have been worthwhile.

Knebworth, a house in Hertfordshire that has acquired romantic associations because of its Gothic and neo-Gothic architecture and its history as the home of a Victorian novelist (Edward Bulwer-Lytton, 1803–73), has been in the Lytton family since 1490. It derives income from visitors, but also from attractions in its grounds (there is a dinosaur park as well as a miniature railway) and from hosting events. There are classic car rallies, and salvage fairs at which the public can pick over architectural curiosities. Most significantly, perhaps, Knebworth has become synonymous with rock concerts – it now styles itself 'The Stately Home of Rock' – the first of which took place there in 1974. Its grounds have hosted crowds of over 30,000, assembled to listen to groups like Led Zeppelin, Pink Floyd, Queen, Dire Straits and the Beach Boys. The most valuable artefact in the house is apparently not a painting, a sculpture or a volume in the library. It is, according to the present owner, a pair of Mick Jagger's underpants that were left behind after one such concert, for the Rolling Stones too played there, in 1974. 'We keep them in the safe,' he says.

Knebworth, a genuine Gothic house that was twice remodelled in the nineteenth century to make it look *more* Gothic, has a delightfully idiosyncratic, rather mad-scientist appearance. It has caught the eye of cinema location scouts, as interesting-looking houses tend to do, and has appeared to date in fourteen films as well as in television programmes. Some were less serious than others, such as *The Great Muppet Caper*, released in 1981. The house was, however, used as a substitute for Balmoral in *The King's Speech* (2010) and as 'stately Wayne Manor' in *Batman* (1989). It was the major setting for *The Shooting Party* (1985), in which both interiors and exteriors were seen, and – an absolute guarantee of exposure and fame – a location in one of the Harry Potter films (*Harry Potter and the Goblet of Fire*, 2005).

Many country houses have become film locations and,

since technology made it possible to shoot inside period buildings instead of creating studio mock-ups (the first to do this was *Barry Lyndon*, made in 1975 and featuring Dublin Castle among other places), this trend has increased. For the Merchant-Ivory production *The Remains of the Day* (1993) the scenes set at 'Darlington Hall' were filmed at Dyrham Park in Wiltshire. For another classic country-house story, the murder mystery *Gosford Park*, some exterior scenes were shot at Wrotham Park, Hertfordshire, while indoor filming took place at Syon House in Middlesex, home of the Dukes of Northumberland whose main residence, Alnwick Castle, has also been extensively seen on screen.

Television can also be a godsend to the owners of country houses, as can be seen by the use of Highclere Castle as the location for *Downton Abbey*. Osterley Park, an Adam house in Middlesex, was convenient for both film and television studios, and was used so extensively as a location throughout the 1960s and 70s that audiences became positively bored by the sight of it (it featured, for instance, as Lord Brett Sinclair's – Roger Moore's – ancestral home in *The Persuaders*).

The future, in a country seemingly obsessed with leisure and dismissed by some critics as a 'historical theme park' is in making the houses – or rather their grounds – fun to visit. Knebworth's Dinosaur Trail is simply one of many visitor attractions that can make a country house more like Legoland than the British Museum. This notion has been taken to extremes at one house, the no-longer-inhabited Alton Towers in Staffordshire. Such fairground attractions are unarguably vulgar, but they can always be dismantled by future generations if fashions change or wealth increases, and if they have enabled historic houses to survive in a difficult economic climate, the sacrifice of some dignity will have been worthwhile.

Old houses cost more than new ones to maintain and repair. If they are also very big houses, these are even more expensive. In fact the cost is three to four times as much. Flat roofs, whether on Elizabethan Hardwick Hall or twentieth-century Castle Drogo, are extremely expensive to conserve. The materials from which a house is built, though no doubt they reflected considerable prestige at the time, now mean that any faithful restoration can be prohibitively costly. The interior fittings – and one has only to think of the elaborate rococo plasterwork in some saloons or dining rooms – cannot by definition be looked after except by craftspeople skilled in this medium. With furniture it will be the same situation, though at least this can be sold and the problem solved. For houses that suffer terminal decline it is usually a matter of selling the contents first and hanging on to the building itself for as long as possible.

For owners who do not have houses that are sufficiently historic or beautiful enough to attract either the paying public or camera crews, maintenance can be a terrible struggle. Even those with both charm and interest can fall victim to impossibly high running costs. In 2009 Noseley Hall, ancestral home of the Hazlerigg family (which had lived there in unbroken succession since 1419), was put on the market by the current head of the family, even though the grounds included the nearby chapel in which his ancestors were buried. It must be agonizing to be the one who must call an end to such a heritage, yet those who inherit such a responsibility often cannot make any career for themselves because their whole lives must be devoted to maintaining their homes, running their estates and providing work for those who live on them. For people in the area the pain of such a loss can be almost as great as it is for the family themselves, but it is easy to see how, once the awful decision has been made and the sale has gone through, there will be a considerable measure of relief as well as sadness.

Since governments, even if they are egalitarian in hue, tend to accept that, as one organization's website puts it: 'private owners remain the most economic and effective guardians of these properties', there is often funding available to help with the upkeep of these houses. Country estates do not as a rule come cheap, and the National Trust does not necessarily have the money simply to buy one. As was seen in the case of Tyntesfield in 2002, there must sometimes be a scramble to raise funds. If this cannot be done, or done in time, a whole heritage can be lost.

The passing of ownership to the National Trust can come as a godsend to proprietors who know that the contents of their family home will be kept intact forever, but it is not always such a blessing. Sir Francis Dashwood, heir to West Wycombe Park in Buckingham-shire, was horrified to learn from his father, after the fact, that the house had been offered to the Trust and accepted. The younger man could have afforded to run the house, and it need not have been given away after all. Once a house becomes the property of this organization the family themselves may well be able to continue living there by arrangement, but there are usually restrictions regarding what they can do and what rooms or facilities they can use. The owner of Brympton d'Evercy, a glorious house in Somerset, expressed a view shared by many others when he said that: 'My chief objection is that there is no way of ever getting the property back once you have given it over. My grandson or daughter could make a million or two at the pools or dealing in African cocoa futures. But there is no way of getting the house back or even of getting a guarantee of becoming a tenant.'

There is also the Historic Houses Association. This exists to advise owners of houses that are still privately owned, and represents about 1,500 such properties (a figure that is more than double the number cared for by the National Trust and English Heritage put together). For houses too remote to attract visitors, too small to accommodate streams of visitors or unable to pay for the necessary Health and Safety precautions, such a body is of vital importance.

Despite their architectural or historical value, the best thing to do with a country house that is too expensive to maintain and too impractical to live in may well be to abandon it to its fate. Once it is roofless, Council Tax (formerly rates) no longer needs to be paid, and some owners have resorted to this. The elements will swiftly reduce even a mansion to a ruin, though it is easier to have it demolished outright. Kilmaron Castle in Fife, for instance, was built in 1820, became derelict after the 1960s, and was finally destroyed in 1984 because the remains had become dangerous. Rather than pay for demolition, the Royal Engineers were invited to blow it up as a training exercise.

In the last 200 years, 1,800 country houses have vanished from the British landscape through neglect, decay and demolition, some of them lamented. Of those that remain, by no means all are worth saving or investing in. But those that offer something, not only the splendour of their architecture, surroundings and contents, but the atmosphere – indefinable yet pervasive – of a way of life refined to near-perfection over centuries of peace and stability, deserve our love, our loyalty and our protection. Not only their beleaguered owners but all who appreciate beauty and history must fight for the stately homes of England.